Modelling Trends and Cycles in Economic Time Series

Palgrave Texts in Econometrics

Series Editor: **Kerry Patterson**

Titles include:

Simon P. Burke and John Hunter
MODELLING NON-STATIONARY ECONOMIC TIME SERIES

Terence C. Mills
MODELLING TRENDS AND CYCLES IN ECONOMIC TIME SERIES

Kerry Patterson
UNIT ROOTS IN ECONOMIC TIME SERIES

Jan Podivinsky
MODELLING VOLATILITY

Palgrave Texts in Econometrics
Series Standing Order ISBN 1–4039–0172–4 hardback
Series Standing Order ISBN 1–4039–0173–2 paperback
(outside North America only)

You can receive future titles in this series as they are published by placing a standing order. Please contact your bookseller or, in case of difficulty, write to us at the address below with your name and address, the title of the series and an ISBN quoted above.

Customer Services Department, Macmillan Distribution Ltd, Houndmills, Basingstoke, Hampshire RG21 6XS, England

Modelling Trends and Cycles in Economic Time Series

Terence C. Mills
Professor of Applied Statistics and Econometrics
Department of Economics
Loughborough University

First published 2003 by
PALGRAVE MACMILLAN
Houndmills, Basingstoke, Hampshire RG21 6XS and
175 Fifth Avenue, New York, N.Y. 10010
Companies and representatives throughout the world

PALGRAVE MACMILLAN is the global academic imprint of the Palgrave Macmillan division of St. Martin's Press, LLC and of Palgrave Macmillan Ltd. Macmillan® is a registered trademark in the United States, United Kingdom and other countries. Palgrave is a registered trademark in the European Union and other countries.

ISBN 1–4039–0208–9 hardback
ISBN 1–4039–0209–7 paperback

This book is printed on paper suitable for recycling and made from fully managed and sustained forest sources.

A catalogue record for this book is available from the British Library

Library of Congress Cataloging-in-Publication Data
Mills, Terence C.
    Modelling trends and cycles in economic time series/Terence C. Mills.
        p. cm. – (Palgrave texts in econometrics)
    Includes bibliographical references and index.
    ISBN 1–4039–0208–9
    1. Business cycles–Econometric models. I. Title. II. Series.
HB3711.M477 2003
338.5'4–dc21
                                                    2002193083

Printed and bound in Great Britain by
Antony Rowe Ltd, Chippenham and Eastbourne

Contents

List of Tables and Figures

Tables

Figures

ix

Series Editor's Foreword

The pace of developments in econometrics has made it increasingly difficult for students and professionals alike to be aware of what is important and likely to be lasting in theory and practical applications. While textbooks in econometrics have expanded in length to cope with some of these developments, there is still an urgent need to be able to focus on particular areas of interest. This suggests a change in format, from a textbook, which covers many areas in some detail, to individual, dedicated and shorter books designed to cover important key developments within a unified framework. This is the essential motivation for the Palgrave Texts in Econometrics, inaugurated with this volume by Professor Terence C. Mills.

This new series will be of interest to students and professionals who need to be able to keep up with the econometric developments. These books are written for a wide audience, with a style that is designed to make econometric concepts available to economists who are not econometricians. For example, the concepts of economic trend and cycle are of interest to general economists and those who are studying, or need to be briefed on developments in, macroeconomics.

The individual volumes are organised within unifying themes. The first theme is that of nonstationarity, which has been *the* major area of development in econometrics since the 1980s, and comprises four volumes. I am very pleased to open the series with *Modelling Trends and Cycles in Economic Time Series*. Professor Mills brings an internationally established reputation as a research scholar and textbook writer to the series. His textbook *The Econometric Modelling of Financial Time Series* (1990, 1998) is acknowledged as a model for clarity and coverage of a vast area. These qualities are conveyed *par excellence* in this book, which brings together developments starting at the beginning of the twentieth century through to the most recent concepts and applications. In addition, Professor Mills provides examples based on the EVIEWS econometric package, which enables readers to reproduce a number of the illustrative empirical examples included in the book. Each chapter also includes a summary of the most important literature, thus providing directed further reading.

Other books within the first theme of nonstationarity will cover the following: testing for unit roots in univariate economic time series; modelling multivariate systems of equations for integrated variables; and modelling stochastic volatility in economic time series. The second theme will cover developments in financial econometrics, an area that was barely in existence a few years ago but which now accounts for some of the most important developments in econometrics. Planned volumes will cover developments in exchange-rate modelling, asset and option pricing and interest-rate determination.

KERRY PATTERSON
University of Reading, England

1
Introduction

1.1 Historical perspective

Modelling trends and cycles in time series has a long history in empirical economics, stretching back to the latter part of the nineteenth century. Until then, few economists recognised the existence of regular cycles in economic activity nor the presence of longer-term, secular movements. Rather than cycles, they tended to think in terms of 'crises', used to mean either a financial panic or a period of deep depression. The early studies of business cycles, notably the Sunspot and Venus theories of Jevons and Moore and the rather more conventional credit cycle theory of Jugler, are discussed in detail in Morgan (1990). The analysis of secular movements was even rarer, a notable example being Poynting (1884), who was the first to introduce moving averages. Although such movements are nowadays typically referred to as trends, the term 'trend' was coined only in 1901 by Hooker (1901) when analysing British import and export data. The early attempts to take into account trend movements, typically by detrending using simple moving averages or graphical interpolation, are analysed by Klein (1997).

The first quarter of the twentieth century saw great progress in business cycle research, most notably in the two groundbreaking books of Mitchell (1913, 1927) and in the periodogram studies of weather and harvest cycles by Beveridge (1920, 1921). Trends, on the other hand, were usually isolated only so that they could be eliminated. This was still typically achieved by modelling the trend as a moving average spanning the period of the cycle, or by fitting a trend line or some other simple deterministic function of time. A notable example of this approach was Kitchin (1923), in which both cyclical and trend movements in data taken from the United States and Great Britain over the period from 1800 were analysed. Kitchin concluded that business cycles averaged forty months in length (the Kitchin cycle) and that trade cycles were aggregates of typically two, and sometimes three, of these business cycles. Of equal interest is his conclusion that there had been several trend breaks – the final one, marking the commencement of a downward trend, occurring in 1920. A later study of secular trend, by Frickey (1934), gives a taste of the variety of methods then available for fitting trends, with twenty-three different methods used to fit a trend to pig-iron production from 1854 to 1926. Cycles were then constructed by residual, producing average cycles ranging in length from 3.3 to forty-five years, thus showing how the observed properties of cyclical fluctuations could be totally dependent on the type of function used to detrend the observed data.

This research was primarily descriptive and statistical. The late 1930s, however, saw the development of formal models of cyclical fluctuations in the economy. Three classic examples were Samuelson's (1939) analysis of the interactions between the multiplier and the accelerator using solutions to difference equations, Kaldor's (1940) primarily diagrammatic, but nonlinear, model of the trade cycle, and Metzler (1941) who, using techniques similar to Samuelson, investigated the role of cyclical fluctuations in inventories in producing business cycles.

While these theoretical developments were taking place, various critiques of business cycle research were being formulated. These took several forms, beginning with the use of statistical analysis to attack the very foundations of business cycles. Fisher (1925) investigated whether fluctuations in the price of the dollar were a primary cause of trade fluctuations. He was particularly innovative in the statistical techniques that he used, as he was the first to introduce *distributed lag structures* into regression analysis. Fisher argued that, because of the high correlation between price changes and subsequent movements in trade volumes and the lack of cycles in the residuals from this relationship, the business cycle as a normal set of ups and downs in the economy did not exist. Unfortunately, the sample used by Fisher, 1915–1923, was probably too short to warrant such conclusions and subsequent reworking of the data by Hendry and Morgan (1995, p. 45–48) suggests that his statistical techniques, although undeniably innovative, were somewhat flawed and do not support the conclusions that he claimed to have reached.

Further difficulties with analysing economic data that appeared to exhibit cyclical behaviour were emphasised by the research of Yule (1926, 1927) and Slutsky ([1927] 1937). The former papers showed that uncritical use of correlation and harmonic analysis, both very popular at the time, was rather dangerous, as ignoring serial correlation in, and random disturbances to, time series could easily lead to erroneous claims of significance and evidence of harmonic motion. Slutsky investigated a more fundamental problem – that observed cycles in a time series could be caused entirely by the cumulation of random events. Slutsky's research was not primarily aimed at analysing business cycles, but Kuznets (1929) took up this issue, using simulation and graphical techniques to explore which shapes of distributions of random causes, which periods of moving averages, and which weighting systems produced the most cyclical effects. Indeed, Kuznets pointed out that this analysis not only removed the necessity for having a periodic cause for economic cycles, but could also make further discussion of the causes of business cycles superfluous.

These studies paved the way for the first detailed *macrodynamic* models of the business cycle to be developed. Frisch's (1933) 'rocking horse theory' of the business cycle, which became very influential, was built on the ideas of Yule and Slutsky (see also Frisch, 1939). Frisch was also keen to suggest that the parameters of business cycles models should be estimated using real data, rather than being chosen by guesswork, and this suggestion was taken up by Tinbergen, who built and estimated the first macrodynamic models of the business cycle, using techniques expounded in detail in Tinbergen (1939a). A model of the Dutch economy appeared first (Tinbergen, 1937), to be joined later by models of the United States (Tinbergen, 1939b) and the United Kingdom (Tinbergen, 1951). While Tinbergen's Dutch model made little impact, his first report for the League of Nations (Tinbergen, 1939a) provoked a long-lasting discussion on the role of econometrics in the testing of economic theory. This debate was sparked off by Maynard Keynes' famous review in the *Economic Journal* (Keynes, 1939). To those economists who had not read Tinbergen's report and who remained ignorant of developments in econometrics since the mid-1920s, Keynes' review must have represented a devastating criticism. After the publication of Tinbergen's (1940) response, and subsequent contributions by Tinbergen (1942) and Haavelmo (1943), a different view began to take hold. As Hendry and Morgan (1995, p. 54) later remark, 'the first suspicion is that Keynes might have been reading another book altogether, or at least did not read all of the book', something that Tinbergen suggested in his reply! While there were many difficulties in empirically implementing econometric models of the business cycle, Tinbergen's research was a tremendous step forward and laid the foundation for much of the macromodelling that subsequently took place.

1946 saw the publication of Burns and Mitchell's magnum opus for the National Bureau of Economic Research (NBER), in which they produced a new set of statistical measures of the business cycle, known as *specific cycles* and *reference cycles*, and used these to test a number of hypotheses about the long-term behaviour of economic cycles (Burns and Mitchell, 1946). This volume created a great deal of interest and provoked the review of Koopmans (1947), which initiated the famous 'Measurement without theory' debate in which he accused Burns and Mitchell of trying to measure economic cycles without having any economic theory about how the cycle worked. Koopmans' review in turn produced Vining's (1949) defence of the Burns and Mitchell position, in which he charged Koopmans with arguing from a rather narrow methodological position, that associated with the 'Cowles group' of econometricians then based in Chicago, which had yet to demonstrate any success in actual empirical research.

Although the 'Measurement without theory' debate obviously focused on the measurement and theoretical modelling of business cycles, some disquiet had also been revealed, particularly by Ames (1948), about the role of secular trends and the methods by which they had been removed before cyclical fluctuations could come to the forefront of the analysis. The appropriate way of modelling trends was later to become a prominent theme in macroeconomic research, but the early 1950s saw theorists begin to work on models in which *trend and cycle could interact*, two particularly influential examples being Kaldor (1954) and Higgins (1955).

The stage was now set for the modern development of theories of the business cycle. Progress was, however, quite limited during the 1950s and 1960s as the sustained growth of the leading world economies drew attention away from analyses of cyclical fluctuations and towards those of demand management and fine tuning of the economy. Even a new definition of cyclical fluctuations was proposed – 'growth cycles' – which were the deviations from long-run trends rather than levels of economic aggregates: the distinction between growth cycles and business cycles is carefully pointed out in the major survey by Zarnowitz (1985). The years since 1975, however, have seen several different classes of business cycle models being developed. During the 1970s, a period of great economic and political instability in many western economies, the concept of a *political business cycle* became popular. The original model of this type is that by Nordhaus (1975). The basis of these models is the notion that governments adapt monetary and fiscal policies so as to maximise their chances for reelection, given that the typical cycle is roughly the same duration as the term of office of the policymakers. Prior to an election, the government will do all it can to stimulate the economy. The negative consequences of these policies will not be felt, of course, until more than a year after the election, when they must then be reversed. This suggests that an electoral-economic cycle will be discerned in output and unemployment.

Published contemporaneously with Nordhaus' political business cycle model was the very different approach of Lucas (1975). In this famous application of the rational expectations hypothesis to macroeconomics, Lucas developed a general business cycle theory that adheres strictly to the basic principles of the analysis of economic equilibrium: the consistent pursuit of self-interest by individuals and the continuous clearing of all markets by relative prices. This paper led to a large literature on rational expectations models of the business cycle, which in turn prompted the development of *real business cycle* (RBC) models. This literature is exemplified by Kydland and Prescott's (1982) prototype RBC model, where a single technology shock to the production function is the source of the stochastic behaviour of all the endogenous variables in the model. This model represents an integration of neoclassical growth theory (as exemplified by Solow, 1970) with business cycle theory by replacing the constant returns to scale neoclassical production function with stochastic elements and a 'time to build' technology, so that multiple periods are required to build new capital goods and only finished capital goods are part of the productive capital stock. Long and Plosser (1983) provided a model that is richer than the Kydland and Prescott prototype in that it adopts a sectoral approach to production, with input–output relationships propagating the effects of stochastic output shocks both forward in time and across sectors.

A further class of business cycle models is based on the twin ideas of comovement of contemporaneous economic time series via common shocks (known as factor structure), and regime switching between 'good' and 'bad' states: see, for example, the dynamic factor model of Stock and Watson (1991), the Markov regime-switching set-up of Hamilton (1989), and the synthesis of the two approaches by Diebold and Rudebusch (1996).

Recent years have seen further research areas develop, often in response to popular developments in other disciplines. The 1970s also saw the development of *catastrophe theory*, first to describe biological processes and then to other applications (see, for example, Zeeman, 1977). Varian (1979) used catastrophe theory to examine a variant of Kaldor's trade cycle model, showing that a small shock to one of the stock variables will produce a minor recession in inventories, but that a large shock may lead to such a decline in wealth that the propensity to save is affected and the subsequent very slow recovery can result in a deep depression.

Nonlinearities can occur in business cycles in many different ways. One important form of nonlinearity is that of *asymmetry*. An asymmetric cycle is one in which some phase of the cycle is different from the mirror image of the opposite phase: for example, contractions might be steeper, on average, than expansions. Although such asymmetries were noted by early business cycle researchers (for example, Kaldor's, 1940, model yields asymmetric cycles, while Burns and Mitchell, 1946, actually observed them in US data), methods for formally examining asymmetries have only recently been developed. Neftçi (1984) was the initial attempt, uncovering evidence of asymmetry in US unemployment by using a nonparametric procedure. Stock (1987) extended these ideas to consider whether macroeconomic variables do indeed evolve on a cyclical time scale, i.e., as defined by turning points, rather than by months and quarters – the calendar time scale – or whether they evolve on a different scale altogether. The former view is implicit in the analysis of Burns and Mitchell, but Stock finds evidence that, although US macroeconomic data evolve on a 'economic' rather than a calendar time scale, the estimated economic time scales are only weakly related to those of the business cycle.

As catastrophe theory became popular in the 1970s, so did *chaos theory* a decade later. Chaotic dynamics are nonlinear deterministic movements through time that appear random when subjected to standard statistical tests (see, for example, Baumol and Benhabib, 1989). Brock and Sayers (1988) applied the new tests for chaotic dynamics to macroeconomic data and, although they found much evidence of nonlinearity, no conclusive evidence of chaos was obtained, a situation that remains the case over a decade later. The duration dependence of business cycles has also been investigated. *Duration dependence* is the idea that expansions and contractions die of old age, i.e., that business cycle regimes are more likely to end as they get longer, so that business cycle lengths tend to cluster around a certain duration, a notion of periodicity that was long implicit in the traditional business cycle literature (see, for example, Diebold and Rudebusch, 1990).

Until fairly recently, business cycle research still tended to mention the presence of long-term trends almost in passing. As mentioned earlier, a not too distorted caricature is that data needs only to be detrended by a simple and readily available method so that attention can quickly focus on the much more interesting aspects of cyclical fluctuations. Although there are some notable exceptions, this approach is justifiable only if there is indeed little interaction between the trend growth of an economy and its short-run fluctuations. Even then, instability in the trend component and/or the use of an incorrect procedure for detrending will complicate the separation of trend from cycle. With the development of growth theory, some attention began to focus on the modelling of trends, with Klein and Kosobud (1961) representing an innovative attempt at fitting trends not just to individual series, but to certain of their ratios – the 'great ratios' of growth theory. This paper is arguably a forerunner of the idea of common trends underlying the concept of *cointegration*, which plays such a pivotal role in modern time series econometrics, as exemplified by, for example, Banerjee *et al.* (1993).

Klein and Kosobud restrict attention to linear, or log-linear, trends, and this was a common assumption for much of the 1960s and 1970s. Although perhaps a useful approximation, the assumption of a constant deterministic trend seems somewhat implausible over long historical periods where there are likely to be structural changes in the economy as well as varying rates of factor accumulation and technical progress. It is therefore plausible to entertain the notion of shifts or breaks in trend or even period-by-period random or stochastic trends. Such trend variability complicates its separation from the cycle and incorrectly assuming a linear trend in these circumstances can lead to spurious cycles being introduced (see, for example, Nelson and Kang, 1981). These twin issues – the independence and the variability of trends – has been the subject of great debate since 1980, a debate that was initiated primarily by two papers, Beveridge and Nelson (1981) and Nelson and Plosser (1982). The former focuses on how to separate trend and cycle when the series is generated by an integrated, or difference stationary, process, i.e., one that has no tendency to return to a deterministic linear trend but evolves as a drifting, and possibly correlated, random walk. The latter paper utilises techniques developed by Dickey and Fuller (1979) to test whether time series are indeed difference stationary rather than trend stationary (i.e., ones that do have a tendency to return to a deterministic linear trend). They apply these tests to a set of US macroeconomic time series and find that the evidence is heavily in favour of the difference stationary representation.

Although many researchers embraced the stochastic trends view of macroeconomic dynamics embodied in these papers, not all economists and econometricians were persuaded by a universal finding of difference stationarity in macroeconomic time series (or the presence of unit roots, as it is also called). Alternative testing techniques, usually either small-sample methods (see, for example, Rudebusch, 1992) or those based on a Bayesian perspective (DeJong and Whiteman, 1991), tended to offer evidence more in favour of trend stationary formulations in the Nelson and Plosser data set. Alternative trend formulations have also been considered. One particularly interesting approach in the context of modelling trends and cycles is the possibility that a unit root appears as a consequence of failing to model the underlying trend as a nonlinear, rather than a linear, function of time. A realistic model may be one in which a linear trend is subject to occasional shifts, possibly in both level and slope, that are produced by infrequent permanent shocks that either occur exogenously (Perron, 1989) or can arrive randomly (Balke and Fomby, 1991).

It is now well known that cointegration between a set of difference stationary series results in them being driven by a reduced number of common stochastic trends. For already stationary series, an analogous property would be that a linear combination of autocorrelated variables has less autocorrelation than any of the individual series (in the sense of having an autocorrelation function that decays to zero faster). For example, a linear combination of stationary but autocorrelated series could itself be white noise, in which case we say that the individual series share a common cycle (more generally, a common feature, in the terminology of Engle and Kozicki, 1993). Vahid and Engle (1993) showed how the common trend formulation can be extended to incorporate common cycles, as well as to provide a framework in which both types of restrictions can be tested and imposed sequentially, thus allowing an integrated analysis of trends and cycles to be undertaken.

This recent emphasis on modelling trends has led to a renewed interest in issues of detrending. A formal treatment of the issue casts the trend extraction problem in an unobserved component framework similar to that of Harvey (1985) and explicitly uses signal extraction techniques to estimate the trend and cycle. Although this will produce optimal detrending if the forms of the unobserved components are known, this may be too stringent a requirement in many applied situations. There have thus been various attempts to construct trend estimators that work well in a variety of situations. Perhaps the most popular of these is that proposed by Hodrick and Prescott (1997). Originally circulated as a working paper in 1980, it was eventually published as a journal article some seventeen years later, although by then it had been used in hundreds of applications! This estimator is known as the *Hodrick–Prescott (H–P) filter*, because it is a two-sided weighted moving average (or filter) whose weights are obtained from a particular optimisation problem – that of minimising the variance of the cyclical component subject to a penalty for variation in the second difference of the trend component. The extent of the penalty depends on the value set for the smoothing parameter which appears in each of the weights and which is typically set at 1600 for quarterly data. The *H–P* filter became very popular for detrending data for use in RBC models. A critical aspect of the filter, however, is the nature and properties of the cyclical component that it produces. For example, Cogley and Nason (1995) analyse this aspect of the *H–P* filter and show that it can generate spurious cycles in difference stationary processes, so that the cycles observed in detrended data may simply reflect the properties of the filter and may tell us very little about the properties of the underlying data. Harvey and Jaeger (1993) make much the same point and Osborn (1995) shows that similar conclusions result from simple moving average detrending.

It is important to emphasise that arguments about how to detrend are not equivalent to arguments about what the business cycle frequencies are. In fact, the *H–P* filter with smoothing parameter set at 1600 closely approximates a high-pass filter with a cut-off period of 32, i.e., a filter that passes frequencies up to the cut-off point, which corresponds to the usually accepted maximum length (in quarters) of a business cycle. Baxter and King (1999) develop the theory of *band-pass filters* (filters that pass frequencies between lower and upper bounds: usually taken to be between 6 and 32 quarters for business cycles) and propose an alternative to the *H–P* filter that seems to have somewhat better general properties. Nevertheless, there continues to be considerable debate about the use of filters, and indeed other detrending methods, as the debate between Canova (1998) and Burnside (1998) demonstrates.

Many of the key papers referred to in the above discussion are collected in Mills (2002), while Niemira and Klein (1994) contains a wide ranging discussion of many issues concerning business cycle modelling and Maddala and Kim (1998), for example, provides a full econometric treatment of trending mechanisms.

1.2   Overview of the book

Chapter 2 considers 'classical' techniques of modelling trends, such as deterministic functions of time, including nonlinear, segmented and smooth transition formulations, and moving averages. Autoregressive processes are introduced for modelling a cycle, and some problems associated with these techniques, such as the Slutsky–Yule effect, are discussed.

Stochastic trends are the focus of chapter 3, where the properties and implications of integrated processes are investigated, along with the distinction between trend and difference stationarity. The class of unobserved component models is introduced, and this leads naturally on to a discussion of the Beveridge–Nelson decomposition, basic structural models, and the estimation technique of signal extraction.

Chapter 4 is concerned with detrending using linear filters. Their analysis requires some familiarity with frequency-domain analysis, and the required techniques are provided in this chapter. Filter design is then considered before the popular *H–P*, band-pass and Butterworth filters are introduced and linked to unobserved component models.

In recent years there has been an upsurge in interest in nonlinear and nonparametric modelling in economics. Several of these techniques have been applied to the analysis of trends in time series. Chapter 5 analyses various of the regime shift models that have been proposed for dealing with shifting trends and also considers nonparametric smoothing procedures for extracting trend components.

Up to this point the book has been concerned with procedures that operate on a single time series. Chapter 6 extends these techniques to a multivariate environment, beginning with the concept of common features, before extending the analysis to consider common trends and cycles within a vector autoregressive (VAR) framework. Multivariate extensions of structural models and linear filtering are then considered.

Chapter 7 presents conclusions and suggestions for an appropriate research strategy for modelling trends and cycles.

The techniques are illustrated by a variety of empirical examples and, rather than cluttering the exposition, citations and references to further reading are provided at the end of Chapters 2–6.

2
'Classical' Techniques of Modelling Trends and Cycles

2.1 The classical trend-cycle decomposition

Researchers studying the growth and cyclical behaviour of industrialised economies are immediately faced with the problem of separating cyclical fluctuations from longer-term, or secular, movements. The difficulties in doing this have been well appreciated for many years, but the traditional methods of trend and cycle decomposition were essentially *ad hoc*, being designed primarily for ease of computation without real regard for the statistical properties of the time series (or set of series) under analysis.

Although rarely made explicit in early work, the underlying model in such analyses is typically one in which a time series, y_t, observed over the period $t = 1, 2, ..., T$, is decomposed additively into a trend, μ_t, and a cyclical component, ε_t, which are assumed to be statistically independent of each other, i.e.

$$y_t = \mu_t + \varepsilon_t, \qquad E(\mu_t \varepsilon_s) = 0 \quad \text{for all } t, s \tag{2.1}$$

In this simple model, y_t is often the logarithm of the series under consideration, while the data are usually observed annually. The extension to, say, quarterly or monthly observations with the incorporation of a third, seasonal, component is, conceptually at least, straightforward, although we shall not consider seasonal extensions in this volume.

2.2   Deterministic trend models

2.2.1   Linear trends

The trend and cycle components are, of course, unobservable, and hence need to be estimated. The methods of estimation that have traditionally been employed are termed *ad hoc* above because they do not arise from any formal statistical analysis of y_t or its components. The simplest model for μ_t that we might consider is the linear time trend

$$\mu_t = \alpha + \beta t \tag{2.2}$$

which, if y_t is measured in logarithms, assumes constant growth. Estimation of the regression model

$$y_t = \alpha + \beta t + \varepsilon_t \tag{2.3}$$

by ordinary least squares (OLS) then produces asymptotically efficient estimates of α and β, although the variances of these estimates will be biased unless the errors (i.e., the cyclical component ε_t) are both serially uncorrelated and homoscedastic. Given such estimates $\hat{\alpha}$ and $\hat{\beta}$, the trend component is then

$$\hat{\mu}_t = \hat{\alpha} + \hat{\beta} t \tag{2.4}$$

and the cyclical component is obtained by residual as

$$\hat{\varepsilon}_t = y_t - \hat{\mu}_t \tag{2.5}$$

Note that the trend component will be efficiently estimated in *small* samples, an important proviso given the rather limited number of observations often available on, for example, historical economic time series, only if the cyclical component is, *inter alia*, serially uncorrelated. This is unlikely to be so if cycles are, in fact, present in the data, in which case generalised least squares (GLS) or an equivalent (feasible GLS) technique is required for efficient trend estimation. For example, suppose that

$$\varepsilon_t = \phi\varepsilon_{t-1} + u_t \tag{2.6}$$

where $|\phi| < 1$ and u_t is independently and identically distributed (i.i.d.): detailed discussion of this process is provided in subsection 2.4.1. Combining (2.3) and (2.6) yields

$$y_t = \gamma_0 + \gamma_1 t + \phi y_{t-1} + \nu_t \qquad (2.7)$$

where $\gamma_0 = \alpha(1 - \phi) + \beta\phi$ and $\gamma_1 = \beta(1 - \phi)$. Least squares estimation of (2.7), say by nonlinear least squares (NLS), will provide efficient estimates of α, β and ϕ.

2.2.2 Nonlinear trends

Although the simplicity of the linear trend model makes it a useful pedagogic device, its assumption of constant trend growth can make it unattractive. An obvious relaxation is to consider nonlinear extensions of (2.2)

$$\mu_t = f(t) \qquad (2.8)$$

Selecting the functional form of the trend, $f(t)$, can, however, be a difficult task. The common view of a trend is that it should be a 'smooth' function of time. Although it is difficult to define formally the term 'smooth' in this context, several mathematical properties can be identified. The function should typically be continuous and, in most situations, have a continuous first derivative. However, this is incomplete, as smoothness also suggests that there should be few changes in the sign of the first derivative. One obvious possibility is a polynomial in time,

$$\mu_t = \alpha + \sum_{j=1}^{d} \beta_j t^j \qquad (2.9)$$

Technically, the Weierstrass approximation theorem tells us that any continuous function defined on a compact interval of the real line can be approximated by a polynomial. However, the requirement that there are few changes in sign of the first derivative implies that the order of the polynomial, d, must be kept low. In practical terms, setting d too high will run the risk of 'overfitting': cyclical movements will become part of the trend, which then ceases to be a smooth, only slowly changing, function of time. This drawback also affects other nonlinear trend functions, such as trigonometric polynomials and sinusoids.

2.2.3 Segmented trends and smooth transitions

An alternative approach that generally overcomes this problem is to approximate segments of the trend function by low-order polynomials. An approach of this type once favoured by economic historians was to allow trend growth to vary across cycles, or more generally 'regimes', whose terminal years are chosen through *a priori* considerations. Thus, if T_1 and $T_2 = T_1 + \tau$ are the terminal years of two successive cycles, then the trend growth rate across the regime spanning the years T_1 and T_2 is given by the least squares estimate of β_τ in the regression

$$y_t = \alpha_\tau + \beta_\tau t + \varepsilon_{\tau,t} \qquad t = T_1, T_1 + 1, \ldots, T_2 \qquad (2.10)$$

More efficient estimates of trend growth across cycles can be obtained by extending (2.10) in at least three ways. The first is to incorporate the models for individual cycles into a single composite model, where it is assumed that the end points of the cycles occur at times $T_1, T_2, \ldots, T_m = T$:

$$y_t = \alpha_1 + \beta_1 t + \sum_{i=2}^{m} \alpha_i d_{it} + \sum_{i=2}^{m} \delta_i t d_{it} + \varepsilon_t \qquad (2.11)$$

where the d_{it}, $i = 2, \ldots, m$, are 0–1 dummies, taking the value 1 in the ith regime and the value 0 elsewhere. If the data is in logarithms, then the trend growth rate in the ith regime is given by $\beta_i = \beta_1 + \delta_2 + \ldots + \delta_i$. The second extension is to estimate (2.11) by feasible GLS to take account of possible serial correlation in the error ε_t. This will allow hypothesis tests of, for example, a constant trend growth rate across the sample period ($H_0 : \delta_2 = \delta_3 = \ldots = \delta_m = 0$) to be carried out efficiently.

Thirdly, note that (2.11) does not allow the trend function to be continuous: even if H_0 is not rejected, the presence of nonzero α_is will result in horizontal shifts in the trend. Continuity can be imposed by considering the class of segmented or breaking trend models. Assuming, for simplicity, that $m = 2$, then continuity at T_1 requires that

$$\alpha_1 + \beta_1 T_1 = \alpha_1 + \alpha_2 + (\beta_1 + \delta_2)T_1$$

implying that $\alpha_2 + \delta_2 T_1 = 0$. Imposing this restriction on (2.11) yields

$$y_t = \alpha_1 + \beta_1 t + \delta_2 d_{2t}(t - T_1) + \varepsilon_t$$

In general, a segmented linear trend can be written as

$$y_t = \alpha_1 + \beta_1 t + \sum_{i=2}^{m} \delta_i \varphi_{it} + \varepsilon_t \tag{2.12}$$

where the functions φ_{it} are given by

$$\varphi_{it} = d_{it}(t - T_{i-1}) = \begin{cases} t - T_{i-1}, & t > T_{i-1} \\ 0 & \text{otherwise} \end{cases} \tag{2.13}$$

and extensions to allow for higher-order trend polynomials and, indeed, combinations of polynomials of different orders, are straightforward.

Although the segmented trend (2.12) imposes continuity, it does not impose a continuous first derivative, so that trend growth still evolves as a sequence of discrete shifts: β_1, $\beta_1 + \delta_1$, $\beta_1 + \delta_1 + \delta_2$, etc. A related model, known as the *smooth transition trend model*, allows the trend to change gradually and smoothly between two regimes. A logistic smooth transition trend takes the form

$$\mu_t = \alpha_1 + \beta_1 t + (\alpha_2 + \beta_2 t)S_t(\theta, \tau) \tag{2.14}$$

where

$$S_t(\theta, \tau) = (1 + \exp(-\theta(t - \tau T)))^{-1}$$

is the logistic smooth transition function controlling the transition between regimes. The parameter τ determines the timing of the transition midpoint since, for $\theta > 0$, $S_{-\infty}(\theta, \tau) = 0$, $S_{\infty}(\theta, \tau) = 1$ and $S_{\tau T}(\theta, \tau) = 0.5$. The speed of the transition is determined by θ. If θ is small then $S_t(\theta, \tau)$ takes a long period of time to traverse the interval $(0, 1)$ and, in the limiting case when $\theta = 0$, $S_t(\theta, \tau) = 0.5$ for all t. In this case

$$\mu_t = (\alpha_1 + 0.5\alpha_2) + (\beta_1 + 0.5\beta_2)t \tag{2.15}$$

and there is just a single regime. For large values of θ, $S_t(\theta, \tau)$ traverses the interval $(0, 1)$ very rapidly, and as θ approaches $+\infty$ it changes from 0 to 1 instantaneously at time τT. This model is thus tantamount to the discontinuous segmented trend model (2.11) with one break. If we allow $\theta < 0$ then the initial and final regimes are reversed but the interpretation of the parameters remains the same. The smooth transition has the appealing property that the midpoint of the transition can be estimated, unlike the segmented trend model where the break times have to be determined exogenously. Note, however, that only two regimes are allowed in (2.14), although this is often not a problem as the transition can take some time, thus imparting a smoothness to the trend.

Example 2.1: A linear trend model for US output per capita

Figure 2.1 plots the logarithms of annual output *per capita* for the United States from 1875 to 1994, upon which is superimposed a

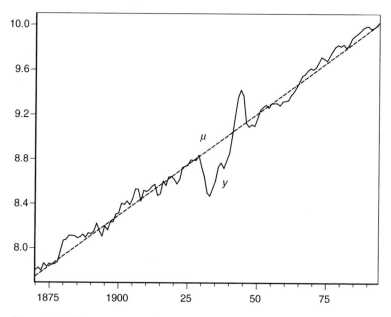

Figure 2.1   US output *per capita*, 1875–1994

fitted linear trend, estimated as $\hat{\mu}_t = 7.75 + 0.0182t$ by feasible GLS using a second-order autoregressive error for ε_t, i.e., $\varepsilon_t = \phi_1\varepsilon_{t-1} + \phi_2\varepsilon_{t-2} + u_t$: such processes are discussed in detail in subsection 2.4.1. Trend growth is thus constant at 1.82 per cent per annum for the whole of the sample period. Although there are major deviations from trend between 1930 and 1950, initially because of the great depression, then as a consequence of the Second World War, the overall fit appears to be satisfactory, with no persistent departures from the underlying trend.

Example 2.2: Fitting deterministic trends to UK output

Figure 2.2 plots the logarithms of annual UK output (real GDP at factor cost) from 1855 to 1999, upon which is superimposed the fitted linear trend $\hat{\mu}_{\text{lin},t} = 3.48 + 0.0181t$, again estimated by feasible GLS using a second-order autoregressive error for ε_t. Unlike Example 2.1, it is clear that this linear trend gives a poor representation of the trend in output, for there are long periods in which the

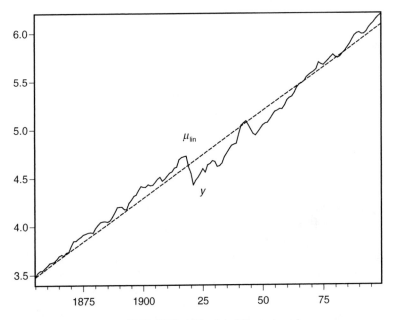

Figure 2.2   UK output, 1855–1999, with global linear trend

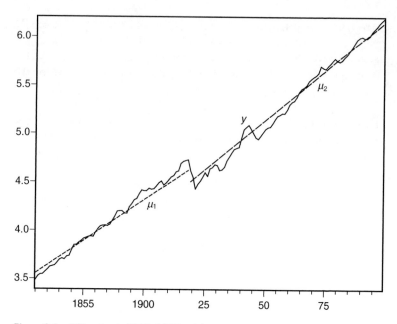

Figure 2.3   UK output, 1855–1999, with separate pre- and post-1918 trends

fitted trend is either consistently above or below output. Figure 2.3 superimposes on output separate trends with a break at 1918, i.e., in the notation of (2.11), T_1 = 1918 and $T_2 = T$ = 1999. These were obtained by estimating (2.11) by feasible GLS, which produced the fitted trend (with standard errors in parentheses and d_{2t} taking the value 0 from 1855 to 1918 and 1 from 1919 to 1999):

$$\hat{\mu}_t = 3.56 + 0.0169\,t - 0.36\,d_{2t} + 0.0036\,td_{2t}$$
$$\phantom{\hat{\mu}_t =} (0.05)\ (0.0012)\ \ (0.10)\ \ \ \ \ (0.0016)$$

Trend growth is thus estimated as 1.69 per cent per annum up to 1918 and (1.69 + 0.36) = 2.05 per cent from 1919 onwards. A test of a constant growth rate over the whole sample period is simply $H_0 : \delta_2 = 0$: the t-ratio of $0.00359/0.00161$ = 2.23 rejects this null with a marginal probability-value of 0.027.

A closer examination of the data shows that there is not a 'clean' break in the series at 1918. Rather, output declines rapidly between 1919 and 1921 before returning to a new trend path. We thus also fitted a segmented linear trend of the form (2.12) with $T_1 = 1918$ and $T_2 = 1921$:

$$\hat{\mu}_{seg,t} = 3.49 + 0.0196\,t - 0.1099\,\varphi_{2t} + 0.1125\,\varphi_{3t}$$
$$\phantom{\hat{\mu}_{seg,t} =}(0.02)\ \ (0.0006)\ \ \ (0.0096)\ \ \ \ \ \ (0.0094)$$

Trend growth is thus estimated to be 1.96 per cent per annum up to 1918, and $(1.96 - 10.99 + 11.25) = 2.22$ per cent after 1921, both rather higher than the analogous estimates from the 'global' linear trend. The fitted segmented trend is shown superimposed on output in Figure 2.4.

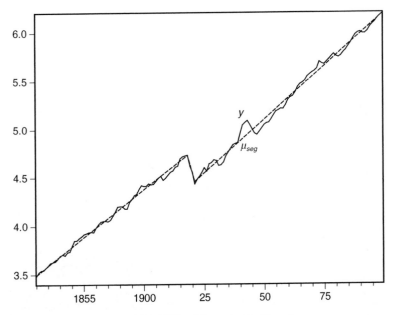

Figure 2.4   UK output, 1855–1999, with segmented trend

A smooth transition was also fitted by NLS, yielding

$$\hat{\mu}_{str,t} = \underset{(0.010)}{3.500} + \underset{(0.0003)}{0.0193\,t} + \left(\underset{(0.024)}{-0.488} + \underset{(0.0003)}{0.0027\,t} \right) S_t(-1.978, 0.444)$$

With $\hat{\tau} = 0.444$, the midpoint of the transition occurs in 1920 and is very rapid. The fitted trend is almost identical to the segmented trend superimposed on observed output in Figure 2.4 and the transition is effectively completed in the two years 1919 and 1920. Note that, as $\hat{\beta}_1 = 0.0193$ and $\hat{\beta}_2 = 0.0027$, trend growth is estimated to be 1.93 per cent in the first regime and 2.20 per cent in the second.

Example 2.3: Fitting a smooth transition to US stock prices

Figure 2.5 plots the logarithms of the nominal annual (January average) S&P stock index for the period 1871–2001. It is clear that a

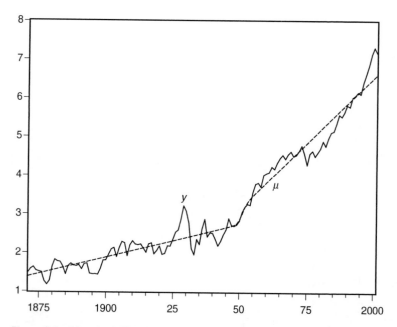

Figure 2.5 Nominal S&P 500 index, 1871–2001, with smooth transition trend

global linear trend is inappropriate and there are no obvious regime shifts. A smooth transition was therefore fitted, obtaining

$$\hat{\mu}_t = 1.389 + 0.0171\,t + \left(-3.638 + 0.0511\,t\right) S_t(1.176, 0.609)$$
$$\quad\ (0.061)\ (0.0014) \quad\ \left(\ (0.318)\ (0.0032)\ \right)$$

Trend growth increased from 1.71 per cent per annum in the first regime to 5.82 per cent in the second. The midpoint of the smooth transition is estimated to be 1951 and, as $\hat{\theta} = 1.176$, the speed of the transition is fairly quick. As can be seen from the smooth transition trend also shown in Figure 2.5, the transition takes about six years to complete.

2.3 Estimating trends using moving averages

2.3.1 Simple moving averages

An alternative method of estimating a trend component is to use a moving average (MA) of the observed series. A simple, equal weighted, 'two-sided' MA computed over an odd number of periods, such as $2n + 1$, is defined as

$$\hat{\mu}_t = \sum_{i=-n}^{n} a_i y_{t-i}, \quad a_i = \frac{1}{2n+1}, \quad i = 0, \pm 1, \pm 2, \ldots, \pm n \qquad (2.16)$$

Note that estimates of the trend are available only for $t = n + 1, \ldots, T - n$, i.e., n observations are lost at the start and at the end of the sample. We shall refer to such a moving average as the (equal-weighted) MA($2n + 1$) filter. For an even number of periods, the MA($2n$) filter is defined using the weights

$$a_i = \frac{1}{2n} \quad i = 0, \pm 1, \pm 2, \ldots, \pm(n-1), \quad a_i = \frac{1}{4n} \quad i = \pm n$$

This filter is defined to have an odd number of weights, with the 'half-weights' for the two extreme observations being the result of ensuring that a trend estimate corresponds to a specific observation.

The MA($2n + 1$) filter (2.16) bears an interesting relationship with the linear trend model (2.2). Suppose we wish to fit (2.2) to the first $2n + 1$ observations on y_t and then use the model to determine $\hat{\mu}_{n+1}$.

We then fit the model to the 2nd, 3rd, ..., $(2n + 2)$th observations and determine $\hat{\mu}_{n+2}$, and so on throughout the sample. In other words, we estimate a 'rolling' linear trend regression with a window length of $2n + 1$. Rather than actually estimate this rolling regression, the trend series can be calculated easily by noting that the parameters of (2.2) are determined by minimising

$$\Sigma_{t=-n}^{n}\left(y_t - \alpha - \beta t\right)^2$$

where, without loss of generality, we take the first set of observations to occur at times $-n,\ -(n-1),\ ...,\ -1,\ 0,\ 1,\ ...,\ (n-1),\ n$. Differentiating with respect to α and β yields

$$\Sigma_{t=-n}^{n}y_t - \alpha(2n+1) - \beta\Sigma_{t=-n}^{n}t = 0$$
and
$$\Sigma_{t=-n}^{n}ty_t - \alpha\Sigma_{t=-n}^{n}t - \beta\Sigma_{t=-n}^{n}t^2 = 0$$

Noting that our choice of observations ensures that $\Sigma t = 0$, and that the trend value that we are interested in is $\mu_0 = \alpha$, the first of these equations thus implies that

$$\alpha = \frac{\Sigma_{t=-n}^{n}y_t}{(2n+1)} = \sum_{t=-n}^{n}\frac{1}{(2n+1)}y_t \tag{2.17}$$

which is the MA $(2n + 1)$ filter. Hence, fitting such a moving average to a series is equivalent to estimating a rolling linear trend with a window of length $(2n + 1)$.

2.3.2 Weighted moving averages

More complicated moving averages result if higher-order trend polynomials are assumed. For example, a cubic trend and a window length of 7 produces a moving average of that order with weights

$$a_0 = \frac{7}{21}, \quad a_{\pm 1} = \frac{6}{21}, \quad a_{\pm 2} = \frac{3}{21}, \quad a_{\pm 3} = -\frac{2}{21}$$

which we refer to as a weighted MA (WMA). In general, the weights of WMAs are such that $\Sigma a_i = 1$ and $a_i = a_{-i}$.

Some well-known trend estimators are obtained by repeated application of simple MAs. For example, Spencer's 15-term MA is the result of successively applying an equal weighted MA(4) twice to an equal weighted MA(5) and applying to the result the WMA(5) filter having weights $a_0 = 1$, $a_{\pm 1} = -a_{\pm 2} = 0.75$. This produces an MA(15) with weights

$$a_0 = \frac{74}{320}, \qquad a_{\pm 1} = \frac{67}{320}, \qquad a_{\pm 2} = \frac{46}{320}, \qquad a_{\pm 3} = \frac{21}{320}$$

$$a_{\pm 4} = \frac{3}{320}, \qquad a_{\pm 5} = -\frac{5}{320}, \qquad a_{\pm 6} = -\frac{6}{320}, \qquad a_{\pm 7} = -\frac{3}{320}$$

The Spencer MA was used to estimate the trend in the early versions of the US Bureau of the Census seasonal adjustment procedure, but was later replaced by the Henderson MA. This is the filter obtained when a cubic trend is fitted by *weighted* least squares, when the weights are chosen to minimise the sum of their squared third differences, i.e., we minimise

$$\sum_{t=-n}^{n} \omega_t \left(y_t - \alpha - \beta_1 t - \beta_2 t^2 - \beta_3 t^3 \right)^2$$

subject to the constraint that

$$\sum_{t=-n}^{n} \left((\omega_t - \omega_{t-1})^3 \right)^2$$

is minimised. Typically n is set at 4, 6 or 12, producing the 9-, 13- or 23-term Henderson MAs. Both the Spencer and Henderson MAs will perfectly reproduce the observed series if it is generated by a cubic polynomial and they were originally designed as acturial graduation (smoothing) formulae.

Example 2.4: Weighted moving average trends for US stock prices

Figure 2.6 again shows the annual logarithms of the S&P index, now with a 13-term Henderson MA superimposed. The weights of this WMA are $a_{\pm 6} = -0.019$, $a_{\pm 5} = -0.028$, $a_{\pm 4} = 0$, $a_{\pm 3} = 0.066$, $a_{\pm 2} = 0.147$, $a_{\pm 1} = 0.214$ and $a_0 = 0.240$. Since six observations are lost at either end of the sample, only the observations between 1880 and 1990 are shown. As the equivalent weights for the 15-term

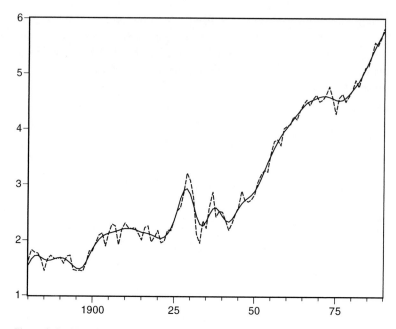

Figure 2.6 Nominal S&P 500 index, 1880–1990, with Henderson MA trend

Spencer MA are -0.009, -0.016, 0.009, 0.066, 0.144, 0.209 and 0.231 (plus $a_{\pm 7} = -0.009$), the two WMAs yield almost identical trend estimates. The trend is very different to the smooth transition fitted in Figure 2.5, and follows the actual series much more closely.

2.4 The cyclical component

2.4.1 Autoregressive processes for the cyclical component

In the trend-cycle decomposition of (2.1), nothing was explicitly stated about the properties of the trend and cyclical components. In the discussion and examples of trend modelling, we have subsequently regarded μ_t as being a smooth function designed to capture the long-run, secular or growth component of y_t. More formal properties will be defined subsequently, but the implicit view of the cyclical component ε_t is that it cannot therefore exhibit any long-run features itself. Consequently, departures of y_t from μ_t must only be temporary, which is tantamount to assuming that ε_t is *stationary*. Put briefly, this requires that the mean of ε_t must be constant, which may be taken as zero here, the variance must be constant and finite, and the covariances between ε_t and $\varepsilon_{t\pm k}$ must depend only on the time shift k:

$$E(\varepsilon_t) = 0 \qquad E(\varepsilon_t^2) = \sigma_\varepsilon^2 < \infty \qquad \gamma_k = E(\varepsilon_t\varepsilon_{t-k}) \text{ for all } t \text{ and } k \neq 0$$

Such a series will then have, by Wold's decomposition theorem, the *linear filter* representation

$$\varepsilon_t = u_t + \psi_1 u_{t-1} + \psi_2 u_{t-2} + \ldots = \sum_{j=0}^{\infty} \psi_j u_{t-j}, \qquad \psi_0 = 1 \tag{2.18}$$

The $\{u_t : t = 0, \pm 1, \pm 2, \ldots\}$ are a sequence of mean zero, constant variance σ_u^2, i.i.d. random variables, so that $E(u_t u_{t-k}) = 0$ for all $k \neq 0$, which we refer to as *white noise*. It is then straightforward to show that the autocovariances are given by

$$\gamma_k = \sigma_u^2 \sum_{j=0}^{\infty} \psi_j \psi_{j+k} \tag{2.19}$$

which allows the *autocorrelations* to be defined as

$$\rho_k = \frac{\sum_{j=0}^{\infty} \psi_j \psi_{j+k}}{\sum_{j=0}^{\infty} \psi_j^2} \tag{2.20}$$

The set of $\rho_k s$, $k > 0$, is termed the *autocorrelation* function (ACF). Stationarity requires that the ψ-weights in the linear filter representation are absolutely summable, i.e., that $\sum_{j=0}^{\infty} |\psi_j| < \infty$, in which case the ψ-weights are said to converge.

Although (2.18) may appear complicated, many realistic models for the cyclical component result from particular choices of the ψ-weights. For example, choosing $\psi_j = \phi^j$ allows (2.18) to be written as

$$\begin{aligned} \varepsilon_t &= u_t + \phi u_{t-1} + \phi^2 u_{t-2} + \ldots \\ &= u_t + \phi(u_{t-1} + \phi u_{t-2} + \ldots) \\ &= \phi\varepsilon_{t-1} + u_t \end{aligned}$$

or

$$\varepsilon_t - \phi\varepsilon_{t-1} = u_t \tag{2.21}$$

This is known as a *first-order autoregressive* (AR(1)) process: recall (2.6). The *lag* (or backshift) *operator* is now introduced for notational convenience. This shifts time one step back, so that $B\varepsilon_t \equiv \varepsilon_{t-1}$ and, in general, $B^m \varepsilon_t \equiv \varepsilon_{t-m}$.

Thus the AR(1) model in (2.21) can be written as

$$(1 - \phi B)\varepsilon_t = u_t$$

so that

$$\begin{aligned} \varepsilon_t &= (1 - \phi B)^{-1} u_t = (1 + \phi B + \phi^2 B^2 + \dots)u_t \\ &= u_t + \phi u_{t-1} + \phi^2 u_{t-2} + \dots \end{aligned} \tag{2.22}$$

This linear filter representation will converge as long as $|\phi| < 1$, which is therefore the stationarity condition. The autocorrelations can be shown to be given by $\rho_k = \phi^k$. The ACF thus decays exponentially to zero for $\phi > 0$, while if $\phi < 0$, the ACF decays in an oscillatory pattern, both decays being slow if ϕ is close to the nonstationary boundaries of $+1$ and -1.

Because of this ACF pattern, the AR(1) process is incapable of modelling the cyclical fluctuations typical of economic time series. An extension to an AR(2) process does, however, allow such fluctuations to be captured. This process can be written as

$$\varepsilon_t = \phi_1 \varepsilon_{t-1} + \phi_2 \varepsilon_{t-2} + u_t$$

or as

$$(1 - \phi_1 B - \phi_2 B^2)\varepsilon_t = \phi_2(B)\varepsilon_t = (1 - g_1 B)(1 - g_2 B)\varepsilon_t = u_t \tag{2.23}$$

where the roots g_1 and g_2 of the associated characteristic equation $\phi_2(B) = 0$ are given by

$$g_1, g_2 = (\phi_1 \pm (\phi_1^2 + 4\phi_2)^{1/2})/2 \tag{2.24}$$

For stationarity, it is required that the roots be such that $|g_1| < 1$ and $|g_2| < 1$, and it can be shown that these conditions imply the following set of restrictions on ϕ_1 and ϕ_2:

$$\phi_1 + \phi_2 < 1, \qquad \phi_2 - \phi_1 < 1, \qquad -1 < \phi_2 < 1$$

The roots can both be real, or they can be a pair of complex numbers, which would produce an ACF following a damped sine wave and hence an ε_t containing cyclical fluctuations. The roots will be complex if $\phi_1^2 + 4\phi_2 < 0$, although a necessary condition for complex roots is simply that $\phi_2 < 0$. When the roots are complex, they take the form $d \exp(\pm 2\pi f i)$, whereupon the ACF becomes the damped sine wave

$$\rho_k = \frac{\left(\mathrm{sgn}(\phi_1)\right)^k d^k \sin(2\pi f k + F)}{\sin F} \tag{2.25}$$

$d = \sqrt{-\phi_2}$ is the damping factor and f and F are the frequency and phase of the wave, these being obtained from

$$f = \frac{\cos^{-1}\left(|\phi_1| / 2d\right)}{2\pi} \tag{2.26}$$

and

$$F = \tan^{-1}\left(\frac{1+d^2}{1-d^2}\tan 2\pi f\right) \tag{2.27}$$

respectively. The period of the cycle is then defined as $1/f$. Higher-order AR models will exhibit cyclical fluctuations as long as they admit a pair of complex roots, i.e., if an AR (p) process can be factorised as

$$\phi_p(B)\varepsilon_t = \left(1 - d\exp(2\pi f i)B\right)\left(1 - d\exp(-2\pi f i)B\right)\prod_{j=3}^{p}\left(1 - g_j B\right)\varepsilon_t = u_t \tag{2.28}$$

A second class of models is obtained simply by truncating the infinite lag order in the Wold decomposition at a finite lag q, thus defining the MA(q) process

$$\varepsilon_t = u_t + \theta_1 u_{t-1} + \ldots + \theta_q u_{t-q} = \theta_q(B)u_t \tag{2.29}$$

It is easily shown that such processes will have ACFs that cut-off after lag q. We may also define 'mixed' models: the ARMA (p, q) process takes the form

$$\phi_p(B)\varepsilon_t = \theta_q(B)u_t \tag{2.30}$$

2.4.2 Estimating the cyclical component

The typical procedure for estimating the cyclical component is simply to calculate it as the residual left after fitting a trend model, i.e., as

$$\hat{\varepsilon}_t = y_t - \hat{\mu}_t \tag{2.31}$$

Having obtained this estimated series, autoregressive models may then be fitted to it. Alternatively, the trend model and the autoregressive error process may be estimated jointly by NLS.

Example 2.5: The cyclical component of US output per capita

Figure 2.7 shows two cyclical components for US output *per capita*: the cycle obtained as the residual from fitting the linear trend in Example 2.1, and the cycle obtained after removing the trend by a 13-term Henderson MA. The two cycles are markedly different, with the former being dominated by the long swings of the depression of

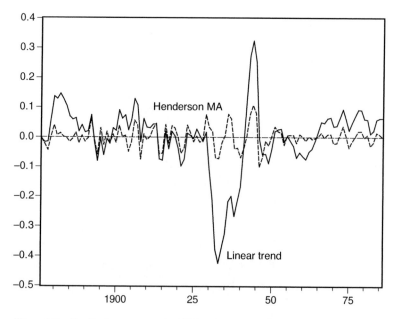

Figure 2.7 Cyclical component of US output *per capita*

the 1930s and the subsequent wartime recovery, and the latter being characterised by more regular cyclical movements with smaller amplitude.

Both series are well fitted by AR(2) processes, these being, respectively, $(1 - 1.157B + 0.335B^2)$ and $(1 - 0.295B + 0.342B^2)$. The 'linear' cyclical component has roots that are just complex, being estimated as $0.58 \pm 0.02i$. This implies a very long cycle with a period of some $1/f \approx 180$ years, which is quite unreasonable and suggests that the series is effectively generated by a pair of identical real roots. The Henderson MA component, in contrast, has roots of $0.15 \pm 0.57i$, which imply a period of $1/f = 4.8$ years, a value that is more consistent with what is traditionally regarded as a 'business cycle'.

Example 2.6: The cyclical component of UK output

Figure 2.8 shows the cyclical component of UK output obtained as the residual from the smooth transition trend fitted in Example 2.2.

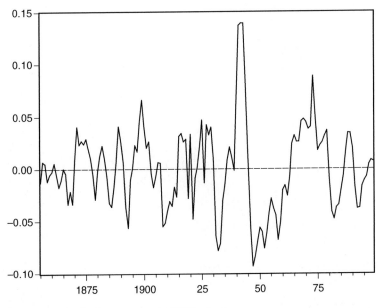

Figure 2.8   Cyclical component of UK output

This cycle is well fitted by an AR(3) process, but with ϕ_2 set to zero as its estimated value was found to be insignificant: $(1 - 0.908B + 0.232B^3) = (1 - 1.328B + 0.558B^2)(1 + 0.42B)$. There are thus a pair of complex roots, $0.66 \pm 0.34i$, along with a real root of $- 0.42$. The complex roots produce a cycle with a period of $1/f = 13.2$ years and a damping factor of 0.75, which has 'superimposed' upon it an oscillating exponentially declining component. The combination of these produces the 'jagged' pattern seen in Figure 2.8.

Example 2.7: The cyclical component of US stock prices

Figure 2.9 shows the 'cyclical' components obtained by residual from fitting the smooth transition trend and the 13-term Henderson MA to US stock prices. The former component follows the AR(4) process $(1 - 0.989B + 0.349B^2 - 0.310B^3 + 0.214B^4)$, which may be factorised as the pair of quadratics $(1 - 1.400B + 0.548B^2)$ and $(1 + 0.420B + 0.380B^2)$. These admit two pairs of complex roots,

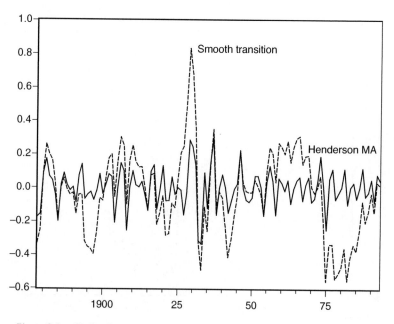

Figure 2.9 Cyclical components for US stock prices

0.70 ± 0.24*i* and −0.21 ± 0.58*i*. The first pair provides a cycle with a period of 19 years, the second a period of 5 years, thus producing the 'long swings' found in this series. The cycle obtained from the Henderson MA is rather unusual, as it requires an ARMA(1, 1) process to fit it satisfactorily. This is given by $(1 - 0.658B)\varepsilon_t = (1 + 0.376B)u_t$. Such a process does not contain a cycle, as can be seen from the rather 'jumpy' appearance of the component.

2.5 Some problems associated with the 'classical' approach to detrending

As the Examples have shown, alternative deterministic trend models must, by definition, produce different cyclical components, and both trends and cycles may have markedly different properties across specifications. We should emphasise that conventional measures of goodness of fit, such as R^2s and equation standard errors, are not appropriate here, as they can be optimised simply by increasing the complexity of the trend specification. Similarly, there are no reliable methods of choosing the appropriate order of a moving average.

Moving average detrending does, however, suffer from a further problem. Suppose y_t is itself white noise, so that $E(y_t y_{t-k}) = 0$ for all $k \neq 0$. Fitting, say, a deterministic linear trend will simply produce a horizontal line after the insignificant trend has been eliminated, leaving ε_t as white noise. However, suppose we fit a WMA($2n + 1$) to y_t, obtaining the trend estimate

$$\hat{\mu}_t = \sum_{i=-n}^{n} a_i y_{t-i} \tag{2.32}$$

If y_t has zero mean and variance $E(y_t^2) = \sigma_y^2$, then $E(\hat{\mu}_t) = 0$ and

$$E(\hat{\mu}_t^2) = \sigma_y^2 \sum_{i=-n}^{n} a_i^2 \tag{2.33}$$

However, the covariances $\gamma_{\mu,k} = E(\hat{\mu}_t \hat{\mu}_{t-k})$ are given by

$$\gamma_{\mu,k} = E\left(a_{-n} y_{t-n} + a_{-n+1} y_{t-n+1} + \ldots + a_{n-1} y_{t+n-1} + a_n y_{t+n}\right)$$
$$\times \left(a_{-n} y_{t-n-k} + a_{-n+1} y_{t-n-k+1} + \ldots + a_{n-1} y_{t+n-k-1} + a_n y_{t+n-k}\right) \tag{2.34}$$

which, because of the independence of the $y_t s$, reduces to

$$\gamma_{\mu,k} = \sigma_y^2 \left(a_{-n} a_{-n+k} + a_{-n+1} a_{-n+1+k} + \ldots + a_{n-k} a_n + a_{n-k-1} a_{n-1} \right) \quad (2.35)$$

Thus the kth autocorrelation of $\hat{\mu}_t$ is

$$\rho_{\mu,k} = \frac{\sum_{j=-n}^{n-k} a_j a_{j+k}}{\sum_{j=-n}^{n} a_j^2} \quad (2.36)$$

and hence, although the observed series is uncorrelated, the estimated trend will be autocorrelated, with nonzero autocorrelations up to $k = 2n$! In particular, ρ_1 will generally be positive and may be quite high, so that the derived trend will be smoother than the original random series and may present the appearance of a systematic oscillation or cyclical pattern. This is known as the Slutsky–Yule effect.

Example 2.8: Simulating the Slutsky–Yule effect

Figure 2.10 shows 200 observations of a simulated (normally distributed) white noise process y_t with mean zero and variance $\sigma_y^2 = 1$,

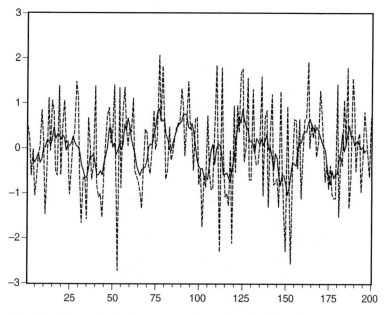

Figure 2.10   Simulated white noise with fitted MA (7) 'trend'

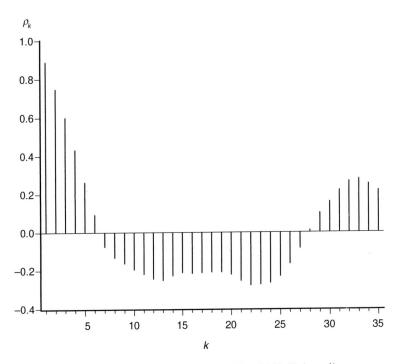

Figure 2.11   Autocorrelation function of the fitted MA (7) 'trend'

with a trend component given by a simple MA(7) superimposed. Application of (2.32) with $a_{\pm j} = 1/7$ for $j = 0, ..., 3$ yields the theoretical autocorrelations $\rho_{\mu.k} = (7 - k)/7$, $k = 1, ..., 6$, and $\rho_{\mu.k} = 0$ for $k > 6$. It is clear that the estimated $\hat{\mu}_t$ is autocorrelated with a pronounced oscillatory pattern and the sample ACF of $\hat{\mu}_t$ is shown in Figure 2.11. The autocorrelations display the predicted linear decline up to the 'cut-off' at $k = 6$, but higher-order autocorrelations are nonzero. This is because the sample autocorrelations of the simulated y_t series are nonzero through sampling error, thus invalidating the independence condition required for the theoretical autocorrelations to be zero, so that (2.34) does not reduce to (2.35).

Further reading and background material

2.1 As mentioned in Chapter 1, the earliest attempts to take into account trend movements, typically by detrending using simple moving averages or graphical interpolation, are analysed by Klein (1997). Such trends were usually isolated only so that they could be eliminated. Even by the time of the studies of Kitchen (1923) and Frickey (1934), trend elimination was typically done by calculating moving averages spanning the length of the cycle or by fitting a trend line or some other simple deterministic function of time. Decompositions of the type (2.1) first began to appear, at least implicitly, in the early part of the twentieth century, often from the perspective of seasonal adjustment: see, for example, Persons (1923) and Yule (1921).

2.2 The linear trend model was typically felt to be too simple for serious empirical work, although it has found its way into time series econometrics as a useful pedagogical device for developing a framework in which to analyse the implications of stochastic versus deterministic trends: see Chapter 3. Analysis of the linear trend with an autoregressive error model of (2.2) and (2.6) goes back to Grenander (1954) and has more recently been analysed in detail in Canjels and Watson (1997), where an extensive set of references may be found.

Greasley (1986), for example, fits models of the type (2.10) to historical output series, while Crafts, Leybourne and Mills (1989) develop in this context the model (2.11). Segmented polynomial trends are discussed in Fuller (1976, Chapter 8.4), where they are referred to as *grafted polynomials*, and their use as trend models was considered by Crafts and Mills (1994a, 1994b) and Mills and Crafts (1996). Smooth transitions were originally introduced by Bacon and Watts (1971), and their use in trend modelling was developed by Leybourne, Newbold and Vougas (1998) and employed by Crafts and Mills (1997). Extensions to two transitions have been considered by Harvey and Mills (2001, 2002a), while Sollis, Leybourne and Newbold (1999) introduce asymmetry into the trend function.

Trend break models were popularised by the work of Perron (1989, 1997), although his focus was on testing such formulations against models of *stochastic* trends, which will be discussed in Chapter 3.

2.3 Kendall (1973) contains a detailed development of moving average filtering. The Henderson MA weights may be found, for example, in Kenny and Durbin (1982), where their derivation is also set out.

2.4 The classic text on time series models of the type introduced in this section is Box and Jenkins (1976). Detailed definitions of the concept of stationarity and the properties of the ARMA class of models may be found in many textbooks: see, for example, Mills (1990, Chapter 2).

2.5 The Slutsky–Yule effect originates in the papers of Slutsky ([1927] 1937) and Yule (1927): in fact, Slutsky was able to mimic an actual 'trade' cycle of the nineteenth century by a moving average process. For a detailed discussion from a historical perspective, see Klein (1997, pp. 276–279).

3
Stochastic Trends and Cycles

3.1 An introduction to stochastic trends

In the absence of any trend component, the observed series y_t would be completely characterised by the cycle (since $y_t = \alpha + \varepsilon_t$) and thus, in general, could be represented by an ARMA model of the form (2.30). The observed series would thus be stationary. We now consider modelling time series that contain *stochastic* trend components and which are therefore generally referred to as *nonstationary* processes.

To this end, we begin by considering again the linear trend model where, for simplicity, the cyclical component is assumed to be a white-noise sequence

$$y_t = \alpha + \beta t + u_t \tag{3.1}$$

Lagging (3.1) one period and subtracting this from (3.1) yields

$$y_t - y_{t-1} = \beta + u_t - u_{t-1} \tag{3.2}$$

The result is a difference equation following an ARMA(1, 1) process in which, since $\phi = \theta = 1$, both autoregressive and moving average roots are unity and the model is therefore nonstationary. If we consider the *first differences* of y_t, w_t say, then

$$w_t = y_t - y_{t-1} = (1 - B)y_t = \Delta y_t \tag{3.3}$$

where $\Delta = 1 - B$ is known as the *first difference operator*. Equation (3.2) can then be written as

$$w_t = \Delta y_t = \beta + \Delta u_t \qquad (3.4)$$

and w_t is thus stationary, since $E(w_t) = \beta$ is a constant.

In general, suppose the trend polynomial is of order d (recall (2.9)) and the cyclical component ε_t follows the ARMA process $\phi(B)\varepsilon_t = \theta(B)u_t$. Then $\Delta^d y_t = (1 - B)^d y_t$, obtained by differencing y_t d times, will follow the process

$$\Delta^d y_t = \theta_0 + \frac{\Delta^d \theta(B)}{\phi(B)} u_t \qquad (3.5)$$

where $\theta_0 = d!\beta_d$. Thus the MA part of the process generating $\Delta^d y_t$ will contain the factor Δ^d and will therefore have d roots of unity. Note also that the variance of y_t will be the same as the variance of ε_t, which will be constant for all t. Figure 3.1 shows plots of generated data for both linear and quadratic trend models. The cyclical com-

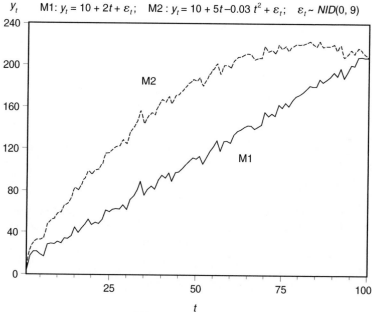

Figure 3.1   Linear and quadratic trends

ponent in both models is assumed to be white noise and i.i.d. normal with variance $\sigma_\varepsilon^2 = 9$, which we denote as $NID(0, 9)$. Because its variance is constant and independent of the level, the variability of the two series are bounded about their expected values, and the trend components are clearly observed in the plots.

An alternative way of generating a trend is to consider ARMA models whose autoregressive parameters do not satisfy stationarity conditions. For example, consider again the AR(1) process

$$y_t = \phi y_{t-1} + u_t \tag{3.6}$$

where, unlike previously, ϕ is now allowed to exceed unity. If the process is assumed to have started at time $t = 0$, the difference equation (3.6) has the solution

$$y_t = y_0\phi^t + \sum_{i=0}^{t} \phi^i u_{t-i} \tag{3.7}$$

The 'complementary function' $y_0\phi^t$ can be regarded as the *conditional expectation* of y_t at time $t = 0$ and, if $\phi > 1$, will be an increasing function of t. The conditional expectation of y_t at subsequent times $1, 2, \ldots, t - 2, t - 1$ will depend on the sequence of random shocks $u_0, u_1, \ldots, u_{t-3}, u_{t-2}$, and hence, since this conditional expectation may be regarded as the trend of y_t, the trend changes *stochastically*.

The variance of y_t is given by

$$V(y_t) = \sigma_y^2 \frac{\phi^{2(t+1)} - 1}{\phi^2 - 1} \tag{3.8}$$

This, too, will be an increasing function of time when $\phi > 1$ and will become infinite as $t \to \infty$. In general, y_t will have a trend in both mean and variance, and such processes are said to be *explosive*. A plot of generated data from the process (3.6) with $\phi = 1.05$ and $u_t \sim NID(0,9)$, and having starting value $y_0 = 10$ is shown in Figure 3.2. We see that, after a short 'induction period', the series follows essentially an exponential curve with the generating u_ts playing almost no further part. The same behaviour would be observed if additional autoregressive and moving average terms were added to the model, as long as the stationarity conditions are violated.

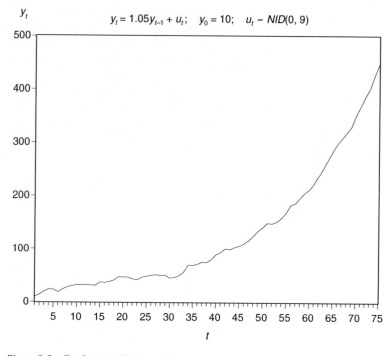

Figure 3.2   Explosive AR(1) model

As we can see from (3.7), the solution of (3.6) is explosive if $\phi > 1$ but stationary if $\phi < 1$, since y_t will converge to zero as $t \to \infty$. The case when $\phi = 1$ provides a process that is neatly balanced between the two. If y_t is generated by the model

$$y_t = y_{t-1} + u_t \tag{3.9}$$

then y_t is said to follow a *random walk*. If we allow a constant, θ_0, to be included, so that

$$y_t = y_{t-1} + \theta_0 + u_t \tag{3.10}$$

then y_t will follow a *random walk with drift*. If the process starts at $t = 0$, then

$$y_t = y_0 + t\theta_0 + \sum_{i=0}^{t} u_{t-i} \tag{3.11}$$

so that

$$\mu_t = E(y_t) = y_0 + t\theta_0$$
$$\gamma_{0,t} = V(y_t) = t\sigma_u^2$$

and

$$\gamma_{k,t} = cov(y_t, y_{t-k}) = (t-k)\sigma_u^2, \quad k \geq 0.$$

Thus the correlation between y_t and y_{t-k} is given by

$$\rho_{k,t} = \frac{t-k}{\sqrt{t(t-k)}} = \sqrt{\frac{t-k}{t}} \tag{3.12}$$

where the presence of two subscripts (compare the definition (2.20)) emphasises that the correlation now depends on t as well as k.

If t is large compared to k, all $\rho_{k,t}$ will be approximately unity. The sequence of y_t values will therefore be very smooth, but will also be nonstationary since both its mean and variance increase with t. Figure 3.3 shows generated plots of the random walks (3.9) and (3.10) with $y_0 = 10$ and $u_t \sim NID(0, 9)$. In part (a) of the figure the drift parameter, θ_0, is set to zero, while in part (b) we have set $\theta_0 = 2$. The two plots differ considerably, but neither show any affinity whatsoever with the initial value y_0: indeed, the expected length of time for a random walk to pass again through an arbitrary value is infinite.

The random walk is an example of a class of nonstationary processes known as *integrated processes*. Equation (3.10) can be written as

$$\Delta y_t = \theta_0 + u_t \tag{3.13}$$

and so first differencing y_t leads to a stationary model, in this case the white-noise process u_t. Generally, a series may need first differencing d times to attain stationarity, and the series so obtained may itself be autocorrelated.

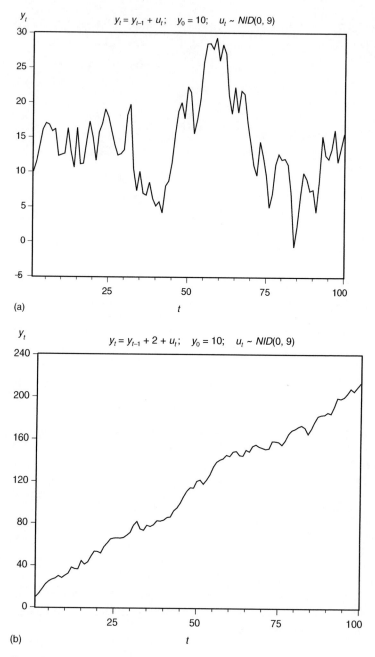

Figure 3.3   Random walks

If this autocorrelation is modelled by an ARMA(p, q) process, then the model for the original series is of the form

$$\phi(B)\Delta^d y_t = \theta_0 + \theta(B)u_t, \tag{3.14}$$

which is said to be an *autoregressive-integrated-moving average* process of orders p, d and q, or ARIMA(p, d, q), and y_t is said to be integrated of order d, denoted $I(d)$.

It will usually be the case that the order of integration, d, or, equivalently, the degree of differencing, will be 0, 1, or, very occasionally, 2. Again it will be the case that the autocorrelations of an ARIMA process will be near one for all nonlarge k.

A number of points concerning the ARIMA class of models are of importance. Consider again (3.14), with $\theta_0 = 0$ for simplicity:

$$\phi(B)\Delta^d y_t = \theta(B)u_t \tag{3.15}$$

This process can equivalently be defined by the two equations

$$\phi(B)w_t = \theta(B)u_t \tag{3.16}$$

and

$$w_t = \Delta^d y_t \tag{3.17}$$

so that, as we have noted above, the model corresponds to assuming that $\Delta^d y_t$ can be represented by a stationary ARMA process. Alternatively, for $d \geq 1$, (3.17) can be inverted to give

$$y_t = S^d w_t \tag{3.18}$$

where S is the infinite summation, or *integral,* operator defined by

$$S = (1 + B + B^2 + \ldots) = (1 - B)^{-1} = \Delta^{-1} \tag{3.19}$$

Equation (3.18) implies that y_t can be obtained by summing, or 'integrating', the stationary process w_t d times, hence the term 'integrated process'.

This type of nonstationary behaviour is known as *homogenous nonstationarity*, and it is important to discuss why this form of non-stationarity is felt to be useful in describing the behaviour of many economic time series. Consider again the first-order autoregressive process (3.6). A basic characteristic of the AR(1) model is that, for both $|\phi| < 1$ and $|\phi| > 1$, the local behaviour of a series generated from the model is heavily dependent upon the level of y_t. For many economic series, however, local behaviour appears to be roughly independent of level, and this is what we mean by homogenous nonstationarity.

If we want to use ARMA models for which the behaviour of the process is indeed independent of its level, then the autoregressive operator $\phi(B)$ must be chosen so that

$$\phi(B)(y_t + c) = \phi(B)y_t \qquad (3.20)$$

where c is any constant. Thus $\phi(B)c = 0$, implying that $\phi(1) = \Sigma\phi = 0$, so that $\phi(B)$ must be able to be factorised as

$$\phi(B) = \phi_1(B)(1 - B) = \phi_1(B)\Delta \qquad (3.21)$$

in which case the class of processes that need to be considered will be of the form $\phi_1(B)w_t = \theta(B)u_t$, where $w_t = \Delta y_t$. Since the requirement of homogenous nonstationarity precludes w_t increasing explosively, either $\phi_1(B)$ is a stationary operator, or $\phi_1(B) = \phi_2(B)(1 - B)$, so that $\phi_2(B)w_t^* = \theta(B)u_t$, where $w_t^* = \Delta^2 y_t$. Since this argument can be used recursively, it follows that for time series that are homogenously nonstationary, the autoregressive operator must be of the form $\phi(B)\Delta^d$, where $\phi(B)$ is a stationary autoregressive operator. Figure 3.4 plots generated data from the model $\Delta^2 y_t = u_t$, where $u_t \sim NID(0, 9)$ and $y_0 = y_1 = 10$, and such a series is seen to display random movements in both level and slope.

We see from Figures 3.3(a) and 3.4 that ARIMA models without the constant θ_0 in (3.13) are capable of representing series that have *stochastic* trends, which typically will consist of random changes in both the level and slope of the series. As seen from Figure 3.3(b) and (3.14), however, the inclusion of a nonzero drift parameter introduces a deterministic trend into the generated series, since $\mu_t = E(y_t) = \beta_0 + \theta_0 t$ if we set $\beta_0 = y_0$. In general, if a constant is

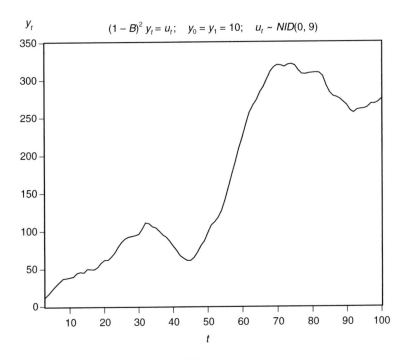

y_t

$(1 - B)^2 y_t = u_t;$ $y_0 = y_1 = 10;$ $u_t \sim NID(0, 9)$

Figure 3.4   'Second difference' model

included in the model for dth differences, then a deterministic polynomial trend of degree d is automatically allowed for. Equivalently,
if θ_0 is allowed to be nonzero, then

$$E(w_t) = E(\Delta^d y_t) = \mu_w = \theta_0/(1 - \phi_1 - \phi_2 - \ldots - \phi_p) \qquad (3.22)$$

is nonzero, so that an alternative way of expressing (3.14) is as
$\phi(B)\tilde{w}_t = \theta(B)u_t$, where $\tilde{w}_t = w_t - \mu_w$. Figure 3.5 plots generated data for
$\Delta^2 y_t = 2 + u_t$, where again $u_t \sim NID(0, 9)$ and $y_0 = y_1 = 10$. The inclusion of the deterministic quadratic trend has a dramatic effect on
the evolution of the series, with the nonstationary 'noise' being
completely swamped after a few periods.

Model (3.14) therefore allows both stochastic and deterministic
trends to be modelled. When $\theta_0 = 0$, a stochastic trend is incorpor-
ated, while if $\theta_0 \neq 0$, the model may be interpreted as representing a

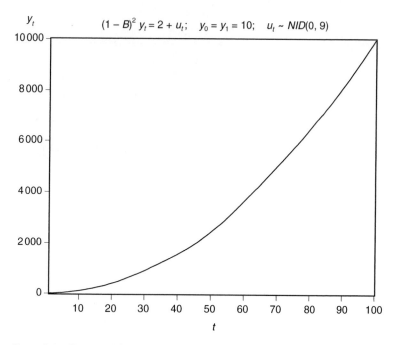

Figure 3.5   'Second difference with drift' model

deterministic trend (a polynomial in time of order d) buried in nonstationary noise, which will typically be autocorrelated. Thus y_t will then contain both deterministic and stochastic trend components. The models presented in Chapter 2 could be described as deterministic trends buried in *stationary* noise: for example, the polynomial trend model expressed as (3.5) can be written as

$$\phi(B)\Delta^d y_t = \phi(1)\beta_d d! + \Delta^d \theta(B)u_t \tag{3.23}$$

the stationary nature of the noise in the level of y_t being manifested in d roots of the moving average operator being unity.

3.2   Determining the order of integration of a time series

As we have demonstrated, the order of integration, d, is a crucial determinant of the trend properties that a time series exhibits. If we restrict ourselves to the most common values of zero and one for d, so that y_t is either $I(0)$ or $I(1)$, then it is useful to bring together the properties of such processes.

If y_t is $I(0)$, which we will denote $y_t \sim I(0)$, then, assuming for convenience that it has zero mean,

(i) the variance of y_t is finite and does not depend on t,
(ii) the innovation u_t has only a temporary effect on the value of y_t,
(iii) the expected length of times between crossings of $y = 0$ is finite, i.e., y_t fluctuates around its mean of zero,
(iv) the autocorrelations, ρ_k, decrease steadily in magnitude for large enough k, so that their sum is finite.

If $y_t \sim I(1)$ with $y_0 = 0$, then,

(i) the variance of y_t goes to infinity as t goes to infinity,
(ii) an innovation u_t has a permanent effect on the value of y_t, because y_t is the sum of all previous innovations: see, e.g., (3.18),
(iii) the expected time between crossings of $y = 0$ is infinite,
(iv) the autocorrelations $\rho_{k,t} \to 1$ for all k as t goes to infinity.

The fact that a time series is nonstationary is often self-evident from a plot of the series. However, determining the actual form of nonstationarity, and thus the type of underlying trend component, is not so easy from just a visual inspection, and an examination of the sample ACFs (SACFs) for various differences may be required.

To see why this may be so, recall that a stationary AR(p) process requires that all roots g_i in

$$\phi(B) = (1 - g_1 B)(1 - g_2 B)...(1 - g_p B) \tag{3.24}$$

are such that $|g_i| < 1$, $i = 1, ..., p$. Now suppose that one of them, say g_1, approaches 1, i.e., $g_1 = 1 - \delta$, where δ is a small positive number. In general, the autocorrelations can be expressed as

$$\rho_k = A_1 g_1^k + A_2 g_2^k + ... + A_p g_p^k \tag{3.25}$$

These will then be dominated by $A_1 g_1^k$, since all other terms will go to zero more rapidly, i.e., $\rho_k \cong A_1 g_1^k$. Furthermore, as g_1 is close to 1, the exponential decay $A_1 g_1^k$ will be slow and almost linear, since

$$A_1 g_1^k = A_1(1 - \delta)^k = A_1(1 - \delta k + \delta^2 k^2 - ...) \cong A_1(1 - \delta k) \qquad (3.26)$$

Hence, failure of the SACF to die down quickly is therefore an indication of nonstationarity, its behaviour tending to be that of a slow, linear decline. If the original series y_t is found to be nonstationary, the first difference Δy_t is then analysed. If Δy_t is still nonstationary, the next difference $\Delta^2 y_t$ is analysed, the procedure being repeated until a stationary difference is found, although it is seldom the case in practice that d exceeds 2.

3.3 Some examples of ARIMA modelling

Once the order of differencing d has been established then, since $w_t = \Delta^d y_t$ is by definition stationary, ARMA techniques may be applied to the suitably differenced series. Establishing the correct order of differencing is by no means straightforward, however. We content ourselves here with a sequence of examples illustrating the modelling of ARIMA processes when d has already been chosen: the suitability of these choices will be examined through further examples.

Example 3.1: Modelling the dollar/sterling exchange rate

Figure 3.6 plots monthly observations of both the level and first differences of the dollar/sterling exchange rate from January 1973 to December 1999, a total of $T = 324$ observations. The levels 3.6(a) exhibit the wandering movement of a driftless random walk: the SACF has $r_1 = 0.98$, $r_4 = 0.90$, $r_8 = 0.79$ and $r_{12} = 0.68$, and thus displays the slow, almost linear, decline typical of an $I(1)$ process. The differences 3.6(b) are stationary about zero and appear to show no discernible pattern. They are very close to being a white noise process, the only (marginally) significant low-order sample autocorrelation being $r_1 = 0.10$. On fitting either an AR(1) or MA(1) process, we find that, although the parameter estimates are significant, the R^2 statistic associated with each model is less than 0.01, which, of course, is approximately equal to r_1^2.

Example 3.2: Modelling the FTA All Share index

Figure 3.7 plots monthly observations from January 1965 to December 2000 of the UK *FTA All Share* index and, as expected,

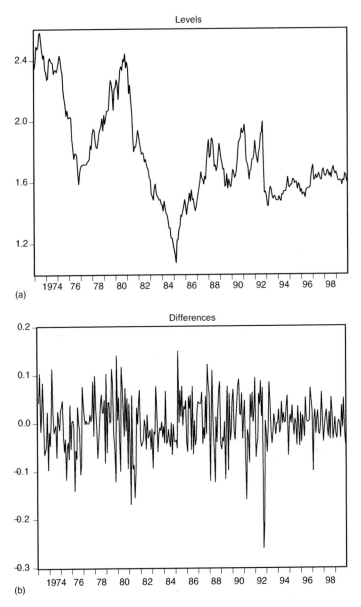

Figure 3.6 Dollar/sterling exchange rate (monthly: 1973–1999)

shows the series to exhibit a prominent upward, but not linear, trend, with pronounced and persistent fluctuations about it, which increase in variability as the level of the series 3.7(a) increases. This behaviour suggests that a logarithmic transformation may be appropriate. The so transformed observations are also shown in Figure 3.7: taking logarithms 3.7(b) does indeed both linearise the trend and stabilise the variance.

The trend may be eliminated by taking first differences, which are well fitted by an AR(3) process. The fitted model is

$$\Delta y_t = 0.0069 + 0.146 \, \Delta y_{t-1} - 0.139 \, \Delta y_{t-2} + 0.105 \, \Delta y_{t-3} + \hat{u}_t$$
$$(0.0028) \quad (0.048) \qquad (0.048) \qquad (0.048)$$
$$\hat{\sigma} = 0.0572$$

The implied estimate of μ is $0.0069/(1 - 0.146 + 0.139 - 0.165) = 0.0078$, which, since Δy_t can be interpreted as the monthly growth of the index, implies an annual mean growth rate of approximately $12 \times 0.78 = 9.4$ per cent. Here y_t is defined as $\log(P_t)$, where P_t is the level of the index, so that $\Delta y_t = \log(P_t / P_{t-1})$, which can be interpreted as the capital gain.

Example 3.3: Modelling US output

Figure 3.8 plots the logarithms of quarterly US output from 1955.1 to 1999.4. Again there is a clear linear trend, leading to consideration of the first differences. Two possibilities suggest themselves, an AR(1) and an MA(2). Estimates of the two models produce identical fits:

$$\Delta y_t = 0.0058 + 0.300 \, \Delta y_{t-1} + \hat{u}_t \qquad\qquad \hat{\sigma} = 0.0091$$
$$(0.0009) \quad (0.072)$$

$$\Delta y_t = 0.0083 + \hat{u}_t + 0.272 \, \hat{u}_{t-1} + 0.139 \, \hat{u}_{t-2} \qquad \hat{\sigma} = 0.0091$$
$$(0.0010) \qquad (0.075) \qquad (0.075)$$

This close correspondence is not surprising, given the approximation between the (inverse of the) AR and MA polynomials from the two models:

$$(1 - 0.30B)^{-1} = (1 + 0.30B + 0.09B^2 + \ldots) \approx 1 + 0.27B + 0.14B^2$$

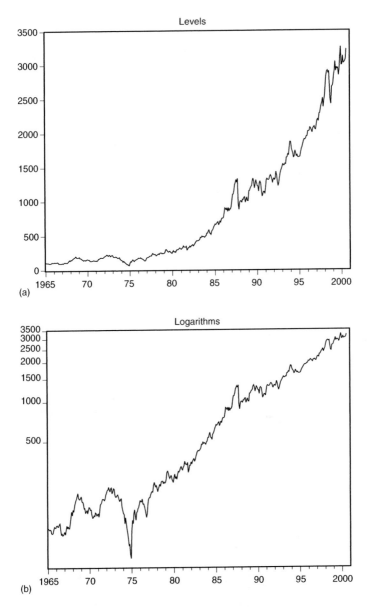

Figure 3.7   *FTA All Share* index (monthly: 1965–2000)

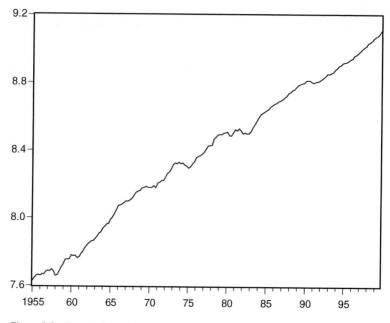

Figure 3.8   Logarithms of US output (quarterly: 1955.1–1999.4)

3.4   Trend stationarity versus difference stationarity

A series generated by a linear trend buried in stationary noise, i.e.,

$$y_t = \alpha + \beta t + \varepsilon_t \tag{3.27}$$

is often referred to as *trend stationary* (TS), in contrast to an $I(1)$ process

$$\Delta y_t = \beta + \varepsilon_t \tag{3.28}$$

which is known as *difference stationary* (DS). Accumulating the changes Δy_t from an initial value y_0 yields

$$y_t = y_0 + \beta t + \sum_{i=1}^{t} \varepsilon_i \tag{3.29}$$

which looks superficially like (3.27), but has two fundamental differences. The intercept is no longer a fixed parameter but now depends upon the initial value y_0, and the error is no longer stationary, for its variances and covariances *depend on time* (recall the special case when y_t is a random walk with drift in (3.11)).

The distinction between TS and DS processes has important implications for the analysis of both economic growth (trends) and business cycles. If y_t is TS then all variation of the series is attributable to fluctuations in the cyclical component, ε_t, and any shock must have only a temporary effect as the series always returns to a linear growth path. If y_t is DS, however, its trend component must be a non-stationary stochastic process rather than a deterministic function of time, so that a shock to it will have an enduring effect on the future path of the series. Hence treating y_t as a TS rather than a DS process is likely to lead to an overstatement of the magnitude and duration of the cyclical component and an understatement of the importance and persistence of the trend component. A related distinction between the two processes is in their forecasting properties. The forecast errors from a TS process are bounded no matter how far into the future forecasts are made because ε_t has finite variance. Moreover, while autocorrelation in ε_t can be exploited in making short-term (i.e., cyclical) forecasts, over long horizons the only relevant information about future y is its trend, $\alpha + \beta t$, so that neither current nor past events will alter long-term expectations. Contrast this with forecasts made from a DS process. Here the forecast error variance will increase without bound, since it is an increasing function of time, while long-term forecasts will always be influenced by historical events through the accumulation of the shocks ε_t.

Given that the properties of the two classes of models are so different, it is essential to be able to correctly distinguish between them. Moreover, the importance of such discrimination is exacerbated by the consequences of incorrectly assuming that a series is TS when, in fact, it is DS. It turns out that it is very easy to mistake a DS process for a TS process that seems to provide a good fit to the data, with a high R^2, small residual variance and significant coefficients, but which generates spuriously long cycles in the detrended data.

Given that modelling a DS process as TS is fraught with potential pitfalls, what dangers are attached to the converse misspecification? Very few, it would seem, for the OLS estimator of β will still be unbiased and will have approximately a normal distribution and, although the efficiency of the estimator is reduced, this will not be serious if the induced autocorrelation in ε_t is simultaneously modelled.

These conclusions are neatly illustrated by the following simulation. Figure 3.9 plots TS and DS processes generated for $T = 100$ by assuming $\beta = 2$, $\alpha = y_0 = 10$ and $\varepsilon_t \sim NID(0, 25)$. (To ease interpretation, we set $t = 0$ as 1900 and $T = 100$ as 2000.) It is readily apparent from Figure 3.9 that the observed TS series is generated from such a process and, indeed, OLS regression of the series on a constant and a time trend yields intercept and slope estimates of 8.68 and 2.01, respectively, and a residual variance estimate of 25.2. Visual inspection of the DS series might also suggest that it too was generated by a TS process. In fact, an OLS regression of the series against time obtains a slope estimate of 1.93, which is accompanied by a t-ratio

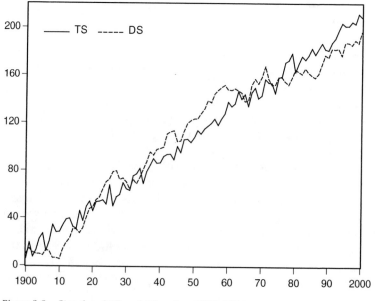

Figure 3.9   Simulated TS and DS series, 1900–2000

of 44 and an R^2 of 0.95! Moreover, the residual variance of the regression is 165, whereas the true error variance of the random walk by the end of the sample should be 2,500. The residuals are also highly autocorrelated, having a Durbin–Watson (DW) statistic of 0.14, and exhibit spuriously long cycles.

The appropriate estimation method for the DS process is to regress the first differences of the series on a constant: OLS yields an intercept estimate of 1.86 with a standard error of 0.49, and an error variance of 23.6. However, regressing the first difference of the TS generated series on a constant yields an estimate of 2.03, thus illustrating how misspecifying a TS process as a DS process nevertheless still enables an accurate estimate of the slope coefficient β to be obtained.

We can distinguish whether an observed time series is TS or DS by computing a *unit root* test. The simplest form of the test takes the DS model as the null hypothesis, embodied in the regression

$$y_t = \alpha + \rho y_{t-1} + \beta t + v_t \tag{3.30}$$

where v_t is a residual, as $\rho = 1$, $\beta = 0$. Assuming ε_t in (3.28) is white noise, then the appropriate testing strategy is to use the standard t-statistic $\tau_\tau = (\hat{\rho} - 1)/s(\hat{\rho})$, where $s(\hat{\rho})$ is the standard error of the OLS estimator $\hat{\rho}$, to test the null hypothesis $\rho = 1$ against the alternative $\rho < 1$. However, the critical values originally derived by Dickey and Fuller must be used, since critical values taken from the t-distribution are strongly biased towards rejecting a DS process in favour of a TS process.

An equivalent way of computing the test statistic is to rewrite (3.30) as

$$\Delta y_t = \alpha + \phi y_{t-1} + \beta t + v_t \tag{3.31}$$

where $\phi = \rho - 1$. τ_τ is then the usual t-ratio testing the null $\phi = 0$ against the alternative $\phi < 0$. Equation (3.31) is often referred to as the Dickey–Fuller (DF) regression. If v_t is autocorrelated, then a sufficient number of lags of Δy_t can be included in (3.31) to render the residuals white noise: such an extension is usually referred to as the Augmented DF (ADF) regression. If β is zero in (3.28), so that there is no 'drift', the time trend can be deleted from (3.31) but the

t-ratio, now typically denoted τ_μ, must be compared to a different set of critical values. For large T, the 5 per cent critical values of the test statistics are –3.41 for τ_τ and –2.86 for τ_μ, as compared to –1.645 under normal conditions.

Example 3.4: Testing TS versus DS processes for UK equities and US output

In Example 3.2 we modelled the logarithms of the UK *FTA All Share* index as an ARIMA(3,1,0) process on noting that it had a pronounced tendency to drift upwards, albeit with some major 'wanderings' about trend. We may thus investigate whether this DS representation is appropriate or whether a TS model would be preferable. Let us therefore test the null hypothesis that the series contains a unit root against the alternative that it is generated as stationary deviations about a linear trend. The ADF regression is

$$\Delta y_t = 0.132 + 0.0026t - 0.029 y_{t-1} + \sum_{i=1}^{3}\hat{\delta}_i\Delta y_{t-i} + \hat{v}_t$$
$$(0.046)\ (0.0009)\ \ (0.011)$$

and it is clear that $\tau_\tau = -0.029/0.011 = -2.76$ does not allow rejection of the DS null. It is therefore correct to treat this series as a drifting $I(1)$ process, rather than as a TS process, which would have been extremely surprising given the implications a TS process would have for forecasting future values of the index!

A question that has prompted a considerable amount of research is whether US output is better represented as a DS process, which we assumed in Example 3.3, or a TS process. The appropriate ADF regression adds y_{t-1} and t as additional regressors to the ARIMA(1, 1, 0) model fitted in Example 3.3, yielding

$$\Delta y_t = 0.299 + 0.00031t - 0.038 y_{t-1} + 0.319\Delta y_{t-1} + \hat{v}_t,\ \ \hat{\sigma} = 0.0090$$
$$(0.132)\ (0.00014)\ (0.017)\ \ \ \ (0.072)$$

Since $\tau_\tau = -0.038/0.017 = -2.22$, it is clear that the DS null cannot be rejected. Note that the fit of this regression is almost identical to that of the previously fitted ARIMA(1, 1, 0) model.

3.5 Unobserved component models and signal extraction

3.5.1 Unobserved component models

When a time series is difference stationary, the decomposition $y_t = \mu_t + \varepsilon_t$ separates the series into a stochastic non-stationary trend, and a stationary cyclical component. Such a separation can be performed in various ways. For instance, a classic example assumes that the trend component μ_t is a random walk

$$\mu_t = \beta + \mu_{t-1} + \nu_t, \tag{3.32}$$

and that ε_t is white noise and independent of ν_t: for example, $\varepsilon_t \sim NID(0, \sigma_\varepsilon^2)$ and $\nu_t \sim NID(0, \sigma_\nu^2)$, with $E(\varepsilon_t \nu_{t-i}) = 0$ for all i. It thus follows that Δy_t is a stationary process

$$\Delta y_t = w_t = \beta + \nu_t + \varepsilon_t - \varepsilon_{t-1} \tag{3.33}$$

Since $E(w_t^2) = \sigma_\nu^2 + 2\sigma_\varepsilon^2$, $E(w_t w_{t-1}) = -\sigma_\varepsilon^2$, and $E(w_t w_{t-i}) = 0$ for $i > 1$, Δy_t has an ACF that cuts-off at lag one with coefficient

$$\rho_1 = -\frac{\sigma_\varepsilon^2}{\sigma_\nu^2 + 2\sigma_\varepsilon^2}. \tag{3.34}$$

It is clear that $-0.5 \leq \rho_1 \leq 0$, the exact value depending on the relative sizes of the two variances, and that Δy_t is an MA(1) process:

$$\Delta y_t = \beta + e_t + \theta e_{t-1} \tag{3.35}$$

where $e_t \sim NID(0, \sigma_e^2)$. On defining $\kappa = \sigma_\nu^2/\sigma_\varepsilon^2$ to be the *signal-to-noise* variance ratio, the relationship between the parameters of (3.33) and (3.35) can be shown to be

$$\theta = -\left\{(\kappa + 2) - (\kappa^2 + 4\kappa)^{1/2}\right\}/2, \quad \kappa = -(1+\theta)^2/\theta, \quad \kappa \geq 0$$

and

$$\sigma_\varepsilon^2 = -\theta\sigma_e^2$$

Thus $\kappa = 0$ corresponds to $\theta = -1$, so that the unit roots in (3.33) 'cancel out' and the overdifferenced y_t is stationary, while $\kappa = \infty$ corresponds to $\theta = 0$, in which case y_t is a pure random walk.

Models of this type are known as *unobserved component* (UC) models, a more general formulation for the components being

$$\Delta\mu_t = \beta + \gamma(B)v_t$$
and
$$\varepsilon_t = \lambda(B)u_t \qquad\qquad (3.36)$$

where v_t and u_t are independent white noise sequences with finite variances σ_v^2 and σ_u^2 and where $\gamma(B)$ and $\lambda(B)$ are stationary polynomials having no common roots. It can be shown that y_t will then have the form

$$\Delta y_t = \beta + \theta(B)e_t \qquad\qquad (3.37)$$

where $\theta(B)$ and σ_e^2 can be obtained from

$$\sigma_e^2 \frac{\theta(B)\theta(B^{-1})}{(1-B)(1-B^{-1})} = \sigma_v^2 \frac{\gamma(B)\gamma(B^{-1})}{(1-B)(1-B^{-1})} + \sigma_u^2\lambda(B)\lambda(B^{-1}) \qquad (3.38)$$

From this we see that it is not necessarily the case that the parameters of the components can be identified from knowledge of the parameters of (3.37) alone: indeed, in general the components will not be identified. However, if μ_t is restricted to be a random walk ($\gamma(B) = 1$), the parameters of the UC model will be identified. This is clearly the case for our 'classic' model (3.32), since σ_ε^2 can be estimated by the lag one autocovariance of Δy_t (the numerator of (3.34)) and σ_v^2 can be estimated from the variance of Δy_t (the denominator of (3.34)) and the estimated value of σ_ε^2.

This example illustrates, however, that even though the variances are identified, such a decomposition may not always be admissable, for it is unable to account for positive first-order autocorrelation in Δy_t. Put another way, such positive autocorrelation implies that, from (3.34), either σ_ε^2 be negative or $\sigma_\varepsilon^2 + 2\sigma_v^2 < 0$! Negative first-order autocorrelation guarantees that the two innovation variances are positive and requires that θ be negative or, equivalently, that the *persistence* of y_t, defined as $\psi(1) = 1 + \theta$, be such that $\psi(1) < 1$. For the general model given by (3.36) and (3.37), it can be shown that an admissable decomposition requires that $\psi(1) = \theta(1) < 1$.

To model positive first-order autocorrelation in Δy_t requires relaxing either the assumption that μ_t is a random walk, so that the trend contains both permanent and transitory components, or the assumption that ν_t and ε_t are independent.

3.5.2 The Beveridge–Nelson decomposition

The assumption that the trend component follows a random walk is not as restrictive as it may first seem. Consider the Wold decomposition for Δy_t

$$\Delta y_t = w_t = \beta + \psi(B)e_t = \beta + \sum_{j=0}^{\infty}\psi_j e_{t-j} \qquad \psi_0 = 1 \qquad (3.39)$$

Since $\psi(1) = \sum \psi_j$ is a constant, we may write, in general,

$$\psi(B) = \psi(1) + C(B)$$

so that

$$C(B) = \psi(B) - \psi(1)$$

i.e.,

$$
\begin{aligned}
C(B) &= \psi_0 + \psi_1 B + \psi_2 B^2 + \psi_3 B^3 + \ldots - (\psi_0 + \psi_1 + \psi_2 + \psi_3 + \ldots) \\
&= -\psi_1(1 - B) - \psi_2(1 - B^2) - \psi_3(1 - B^3) - \ldots \\
&= (1 - B)\left(-\psi_1 - \psi_2(1 + B) - \psi_3(1 + B + B^2) - \ldots\right) \\
&= (1 - B)\left(-\left(\sum_{j=1}^{\infty}\psi_j\right) - \left(\sum_{j=2}^{\infty}\psi_j\right)B - \left(\sum_{j=3}^{\infty}\psi_j\right)B^2 - \ldots\right) \\
&= \Delta\tilde{\psi}(B)
\end{aligned}
$$

Thus

$$\psi(B) = \psi(1) + \Delta\tilde{\psi}(B) \qquad (3.40)$$

implying that

$$\Delta y_t = \beta + \psi(1)e_t + \Delta\tilde{\psi}(B)e_t \qquad (3.41)$$

and, in terms of the trend and cycle components,

$$\Delta\mu_t = \beta + \psi(1)e_t \tag{3.42}$$

and

$$\varepsilon_t = \tilde{\psi}(B)e_t = -\left(\sum_{j=1}^{\infty}\psi_j\right)e_t - \left(\sum_{j=2}^{\infty}\psi_j\right)e_{t-1} - \left(\sum_{j=3}^{\infty}\psi_j\right)e_{t-2} - \ldots \tag{3.43}$$

Thus the trend is a random walk with drift β and innovation $\psi(1)e_t$, which will therefore be proportional to the innovation to Δy_t and will have a variance of $[\psi(1)]^2\sigma_e^2$, which may be larger or smaller than σ_e^2 depending on the signs and pattern of the ψ_js. The cyclical component is clearly stationary, but since it is driven by the same innovation as the trend component, μ_t and ε_t must be *perfectly correlated*, in direct contrast to the 'classic' decomposition that assumes that they are independent. The decomposition (3.42) and (3.43) is known as the Beveridge–Nelson (B–N) decomposition. For example, the B–N decomposition of the ARIMA(0, 1, 1) process (3.35) is

$$\Delta\mu_t = \beta + (1 + \theta)e_t \tag{3.44}$$

$$\varepsilon_t = -\theta e_t \tag{3.45}$$

The relationship between the B–N decomposition of an ARIMA(0, 1, 1) process and the 'classic' UC model, but with *perfectly correlated* innovations, is exact. Rather than assuming that ε_t and ν_t are independent, suppose that $\nu_t = \alpha\varepsilon_t$. Equating (3.33) and (3.35) then yields

$$\Delta y_t = \beta + (1 + \alpha)\varepsilon_t - \varepsilon_{t-1} = \beta + e_t - \theta e_{t-1}$$

so that $e_t = (1 + \alpha)\varepsilon_t$ and $\theta e_t = -\varepsilon_t$, thus recovering (3.45) and implying that $\theta = -1/(1 + \alpha)$. The B–N trend (3.44) then becomes

$$\Delta\mu_t = \beta + (1 + \theta)e_t = \beta - \frac{(1+\theta)}{\theta}\varepsilon_t = \beta + \alpha\varepsilon_t = \beta + \nu_t$$

which recovers (3.32).

A simple way of estimating the B–N components is to approximate the Wold decomposition (3.39) by an ARIMA (p, 1, q) process:

$$\Delta y_t = \beta + \frac{\left(1 + \theta_1 B + \ldots + \theta_q B^q\right)}{\left(1 - \phi_1 B - \ldots - \phi_p B^p\right)} e_t = \beta + \frac{\theta(B)}{\phi(B)} e_t \tag{3.46}$$

so that

$$\Delta \mu_t = \beta + \psi(1) e_t = \beta + \frac{\left(1 + \theta_1 + \ldots + \theta_q\right)}{\left(1 - \phi_1 - \ldots - \phi_p\right)} e_t \tag{3.47}$$

where $\psi(1) = \theta(1)/\phi(1)$ is the persistence measure for y_t. Equation (3.46) can then be written as

$$\frac{\phi(B)}{\theta(B)} \Delta y_t = \beta \frac{\phi(1)}{\theta(1)} + e_t$$

or as

$$\frac{\phi(B)}{\theta(B)} \psi(1) \Delta y_t = \beta + \psi(1) e_t \tag{3.48}$$

A comparison of (3.47) and (3.48) reveals that

$$\mu_t = \frac{\phi(B)}{\theta(B)} \psi(1) y_t = \omega(B) y_t \tag{3.49}$$

which allows μ_t to be recursively estimated and ε_t to be obtained by residual. Note that the trend is thus a weighted average of current and past values of the observed series, with the weights summing to one since $\omega(1) = 1$. The cyclical component is then given by

$$\varepsilon_t = y_t - \omega(B) y_t = \tilde{\omega}(B) y_t = \frac{\phi(1)\theta(B) - \theta(1)\phi(B)}{\phi(1)\theta(B)} y_t \tag{3.50}$$

Since $\tilde{\omega}(1) = 1 - \omega(1) = 0$, the weights for the cycle moving average sum to zero. The cycle can also be expressed as

$$\varepsilon_t = \frac{\phi(1)\theta(B) - \theta(1)\phi(B)}{\phi(1)\phi(B)\Delta} e_t \tag{3.51}$$

Since the cycle is stationary, we can write the numerator of (3.51) as $\phi(1)\theta(B) - \theta(1)\phi(B) = \Delta\varphi(B)$, since it must contain a unit root to cancel out the one in the denominator. As the order of the numerator is $\max(p, q)$, $\varphi(B)$ must be of order $r = \max(p, q) - 1$, implying that the cycle has the ARMA(p, r) representation

$$\phi(B)\varepsilon_t = \{\varphi(B) / \phi(1)\}e_t \tag{3.52}$$

For example, for the ARIMA(0, 1, 1) process (3.35)

$$\mu_t = (1+\theta B)^{-1}(1+\theta)y_t = (1-\theta B + \theta^2 B^2 - ...)(1+\theta)y_t = (1+\theta)\Sigma_{j=0}^{\infty}(-\theta)^j y_{t-j}$$

and

$$\varepsilon_t = \frac{(1+\theta B)-(1+\theta)}{(1+\theta B)}y_t = \frac{-\theta(1-B)}{(1+\theta B)}y_t = -\theta(1+\theta B)^{-1}\Delta y_t = -\theta\Sigma_{j=0}^{\infty}(-\theta)^j \Delta y_{t-j}$$

Equivalently

$$\hat{\mu}_t = \theta\hat{\mu}_{t-1}+(1-\theta)y_t, \quad \hat{\varepsilon}_t = y_t - \hat{\mu}_t$$

Thus, with starting values $\hat{\mu}_1 = y_1$ and $\hat{\varepsilon}_1 = 0$, the trend can be estimated as a weighted average of the past trend and the current observed value, the weights depending upon θ. If $\theta = 0$, so that y_t follows a pure random walk with drift, $\hat{\mu}_t = y_t$ and there is no cyclical component, whereas if $\theta = 1$, the series is stationary, there is no trend and $\hat{\varepsilon}_t = y_t$.

In a more general context, it is possible for any series with a Wold decomposition to be written as the sum of a random walk trend and a stationary cycle and where the innovations of the two components are correlated to an arbitrary degree. However, only the B–N decomposition is *guaranteed* to exist.

Example 3.5: Decomposing UK equities and US output

In Example 3.2 the following ARIMA(3, 1, 0) model was fitted to the UK *FTA All Share* index

$$\left(1-0.146B+0.139B^2 -0.105B^3\right)\Delta y_t = 0.0069 + e_t$$

Persistence is thus given by $\psi(1) = 1/(1 - 0.146 + 0.139 - 0.105) = 1.126$ and the B–N trend is

$$\Delta\mu_t = 0.0069 + 1.126e_t$$

or, equivalently,

$$\mu_t = 1.126y_t - 0.164y_{t-1} + 0.156y_{t-2} - 0.118y_{t-3}$$

The B–N cycle is

$$\varepsilon_t = 0.146\varepsilon_{t-1} - 0.139\varepsilon_{t-2} + 0.105\varepsilon_{t-3} - 0.126e_t - 0.038e_{t-1} - 0.118e_{t-2}$$
$$= -0.126y_t + 0.164y_{t-1} - 0.156y_{t-2} + 0.118y_{t-3}$$

The B–N trend turns out to be almost identical to the observed series, thus leaving only a very small B–N cycle.

In Example 3.3 the following ARIMA(0, 1, 2) model was fitted to US output

$$\Delta y_t = 0.0083 + (1 + 0.272B + 0.139B^2)e_t$$

Here the B–N trend is thus

$$\Delta\mu_t = 0.0083 + 1.411e_t$$

i.e.

$$\mu_t = 1.411y_t - 0.272\mu_{t-1} - 0.139\mu_{t-2}$$

The B–N cycle is

$$\varepsilon_t = -0.411e_t - 0.139e_{t-1}$$
$$= 0.272\varepsilon_{t-1} + 0.139\varepsilon_{t-2} - 0.411y_t + 0.272y_{t-1} + 0.139y_{t-2}$$

Again, the B–N trend is very close to the actual series and, as a consequence, the B–N cycle is numerically small, having a range of approximately ± 0.015.

Although we can decompose both equities and output as $y_t = \mu_t + \varepsilon_t$, where

$$\Delta\mu_t = \beta + \nu_t$$

and

$$\varepsilon_t = \lambda(B)u_t$$

and ν_t and u_t are uncorrelated, such a decomposition will be inadmissable, since $\psi(1) > 1$ in both cases.

3.5.3   Signal extraction

The B–N decomposition yields a trend estimator (3.49) that is *one-sided* in the sense that only current and past values of the observed series are used in its construction. Future values may be incorporated to define the *two-sided* B–N estimator $\mu_{t|T} = \omega^T(B)y_t$, where the filter $\omega^T(B)$ is given by

$$\omega^T(B) = \omega(B)\omega(B^{-1}) = \left[\psi(1)\right]^2 \frac{\phi(B)\phi(B^{-1})}{\theta(B)\theta(B^{-1})} \tag{3.53}$$

For the ARIMA(0,1,1) process (3.35), this estimator becomes

$$\mu_{t|T} = (1+\theta)^2 \frac{1}{(1+\theta B)(1+\theta B)} y_t = \frac{1+\theta}{1-\theta} \sum_{j=-\infty}^{\infty} (-\theta)^j \tag{3.54}$$

The estimator (3.53) is closely related to the Weiner–Kolmogorov (WK) filter estimate of μ_t in the UC model of (3.36) and (3.37). This is given by

$$\mu_{t|T} = \frac{\sigma_\nu^2}{\sigma_e^2} \frac{\gamma(B)\gamma(B^{-1})}{\theta(B)\theta(B^{-1})} y_t \tag{3.55}$$

If the trend is a random walk, so that $\gamma(B) = 1$, then (3.36) and (3.37) imply

$$\nu_t + \Delta\lambda(B)u_t = \theta(B)e_t$$

Setting $B = 1$ yields $\nu_t = \theta(1)e_t$, whereupon squaring and taking expectations obtains $\sigma_\nu^2 = [\theta(1)]^2\sigma_e^2$. Substituting into (3.55) obtains

$$\mu_{t|T} = [\theta(1)]^2 \frac{1}{\theta(B)\theta(B^{-1})} y_t$$

which is equivalent to using the filter (3.53) when $\phi(B) = 1$. Thus the two-sided B–N trend estimator, sometimes referred to as the B–N *smoother*, is shown to be the optimal estimator for a UC model consisting of a random walk trend and an *uncorrelated* stationary cycle, even though the one-sided B–N estimator arises from the same model but with *perfectly correlated* components.

This is an example of the technique of *signal extraction*. For the classic UC model, the optimal trend estimator is thus (3.54). Hence, for values of θ close to -1, $\hat{\mu}_{t|T}$ will be given by a very long moving average of future and past values of y. If θ is close to zero, however, $\hat{\mu}_{t|T}$ will be almost equal to the most recently observed value of y. Values of θ close to -1 correspond to small values of the signal-to-noise ratio κ. Thus when the noise component dominates, a long moving average of y values provides the best estimate of trend, while if the noise component is only small the trend is given by the current position of y.

As noted earlier, if we are given only y_t and its model, i.e., (3.37), then from (3.38), models for μ_t and ε_t are in general unidentified. If y_t follows the ARIMA(0, 1, 1) process

$$(1 - B)y_t = (1 + \theta B)e_t \tag{3.56}$$

then the most general signal-plus-*white*-noise UC model has μ_t given by

$$(1 - B)\mu_t = (1 + \Theta B)v_t \tag{3.57}$$

and, for any value of Θ in the interval $\theta < \Theta \leq 1$, there exists values of σ_u^2 and σ_v^2 such that $\mu_t + \varepsilon_t$ yields (3.56). It can be shown that setting $\Theta = 1$ minimises the variance of both μ_t and ε_t and this is known as the *canonical decomposition* of y_t. Choosing this value implies that $\gamma(B) = 1 + B$, and we thus have

$$\hat{\mu}_{t|T} = \frac{\sigma_v^2(1 + B)(1 + B^{-1})}{\sigma_e^2(1 + \theta B)(1 + \theta B^{-1})} y_t \tag{3.58}$$

3.5.4 Basic structural models

The basic structural model (BSM) defines the trend component to be

$$\mu_t = \mu_{t-1} + \beta_{t-1} + \eta_t, \qquad\qquad \eta_t \sim NID(0, \sigma_\eta^2) \qquad (3.59)$$
$$\beta_t = \beta_{t-1} + \zeta_t, \qquad\qquad \zeta_t \sim NID(0, \sigma_\zeta^2) \qquad (3.60)$$

The trend thus receives shocks to both its level and slope, although these disturbances are assumed to be mutually independent of each other and with the cycle ε_t. If both variances σ_η^2 and σ_ζ^2 are zero, then $\beta_t = \beta_{t-1} = \beta$, say, and $\mu_t = \mu_{t-1} + \beta = \mu_0 + \beta t$, so that the trend is deterministic. When only σ_ζ^2 is zero, the slope is fixed and the trend reduces to a random walk with drift

$$\mu_t = \mu_{t-1} + \beta + \eta_t \qquad (3.61)$$

Allowing σ_ζ^2 to be positive, but setting σ_η^2 to zero, gives an 'integrated random walk' trend

$$\Delta\mu_t = \Delta\mu_{t-1} + \zeta_{t-1} \qquad (3.62)$$

which, when estimated, tends to be relatively smooth, so that this is often referred to as the *smooth trend* model.

With regard to the cycle, suppose ε_t is a cyclical function of time with frequency λ_c, which is measured in radians. The period of the cycle is then $2\pi/\lambda_c$. Such a cycle can be represented by a mixture of sine and cosine waves, such as

$$\varepsilon_t = a\cos\lambda_c t + b\sin\lambda_c t \qquad (3.63)$$

As it stands, (3.63) is deterministic, but it can be made stochastic by allowing the parameters a and b to evolve over time. This may be done by defining the cycle as

$$\begin{bmatrix} \varepsilon_t \\ \varepsilon_t^* \end{bmatrix} = \rho \begin{bmatrix} \cos\lambda_c & \sin\lambda_c \\ -\sin\lambda_c & \cos\lambda_c \end{bmatrix} \begin{bmatrix} \varepsilon_{t-1} \\ \varepsilon_{t-1}^* \end{bmatrix} + \begin{bmatrix} \varsigma_t \\ \varsigma_t^* \end{bmatrix} \qquad (3.64)$$

Here ε_t^* and ς_t^* appear by construction, and ς_t and ς_t^* are assumed to be independent zero mean white noises with common variance σ_ς^2. The parameter ρ is known as the damping factor and, for $0 \leq \rho < 1$, the cycle ε_t is stationary with zero mean, variance $\sigma_\varepsilon^2 = \sigma_\varsigma^2/(1 - \rho^2)$ and ACF given by $\rho^k \cos\lambda_c k$, $k = 0, 1, 2, \ldots$. Equation (3.64) can be written as

$$\begin{bmatrix} \varepsilon_t \\ \varepsilon_t^* \end{bmatrix} = \begin{bmatrix} 1-\rho\cos\lambda_c B & -\rho\sin\lambda_c B \\ \rho\sin\lambda_c B & 1-\rho\cos\lambda_c B \end{bmatrix}^{-1} \begin{bmatrix} \varsigma_t \\ \varsigma_t^* \end{bmatrix}$$

$$= \frac{1}{\phi(B)} \begin{bmatrix} 1-\rho\cos\lambda_c B & \rho\sin\lambda_c B \\ -\rho\sin\lambda_c B & 1-\rho\cos\lambda_c B \end{bmatrix} \begin{bmatrix} \varsigma_t \\ \varsigma_t^* \end{bmatrix} \tag{3.65}$$

where $\phi(B) = 1 - 2\rho\cos\lambda_c B + \rho^2 B^2$. Thus the cycle can be expressed as

$$\phi(B)\varepsilon_t = (1 - \rho\cos\lambda_c B)\varsigma_t + (\rho\sin\lambda_c B)\varsigma_t^* \tag{3.66}$$

which is an ARMA(2,1) process. The AR polynomial $\phi(B)$ has roots

$$g_1, g_2 = \left(2\rho\cos\lambda_c \pm (4\rho^2\cos^2\lambda_c - 4\rho^2)^{1/2}\right)/2$$
$$= \rho(\cos\lambda_c \pm i\sin\lambda_c) = \rho\exp(\pm i\lambda_c) \tag{3.67}$$

which, for $0 < \lambda_c < \pi$, are a pair of complex conjugates with modulus ρ and phase λ_c. Hence this formulation effectively restricts ε_t to display 'pseudo-'cyclical behaviour. For $\lambda_c = 0$, (3.66) becomes

$$(1 - 2\rho B + \rho^2 B^2)\varepsilon_t = (1 + \rho B)\varsigma_t$$

i.e., $(1 - \rho B)\varepsilon_t = \varsigma_t$, while for $\lambda_c = \pi$, (3.66) becomes

$$(1 + 2\rho B + \rho^2 B^2)\varepsilon_t = (1 + \rho B)\varsigma_t$$

i.e., $(1 + \rho B)\varepsilon_t = \varsigma_t$. Thus the limiting cases are both AR(1) processes with coefficients ρ and $-\rho$, respectively.

The BSM defined by (3.59), (3.60) and (3.63) is best analysed statistically by putting it into *state space form*. This comprises the *measurement equation*

$$y_t = [1 \ 0 \ 1 \ 0]\alpha_t \tag{3.68}$$

and the *transition equation*

$$\alpha_t = \begin{bmatrix} \mu_t \\ \beta_t \\ \varepsilon_t \\ \varepsilon_t^* \end{bmatrix} = \begin{bmatrix} \begin{array}{cc|cc} 1 & 1 & & \\ 0 & 1 & & \mathbf{0} \\ \hline & & \rho\cos\lambda_c & \rho\sin\lambda_c \\ \mathbf{0} & & -\rho\sin\lambda_c & \rho\cos\lambda_c \end{array} \end{bmatrix} \begin{bmatrix} \mu_{t-1} \\ \beta_{t-1} \\ \varepsilon_{t-1} \\ \varepsilon_{t-1}^* \end{bmatrix} + \begin{bmatrix} \eta_t \\ \zeta_t \\ \varsigma_t \\ \varsigma_t^* \end{bmatrix} \tag{3.69}$$

Application of the Kalman filter to (3.68) and (3.69) yields estimators of the components based on current and past observations. These are known as the *filtered estimates*, but smoothed estimates, which use future observations as well, can be obtained by running the Kalman filter backwards from the last observation. Estimates of the unknown variance parameters can be obtained by constructing a likelihood function from the one-step-ahead innovations produced by the Kalman filter, which is then maximised by an iterative procedure. Once estimated, standard errors of all parameters can be computed and the fit of the model can be checked using standard time series diagnostics such as tests for residual correlation.

Example 3.6: Basic structural models for UK equities and output

The BSM was fitted to the UK *FTA All Share* index analysed in several previous examples in this chapter. The variances in (3.59) and (3.60) were estimated as $\hat{\sigma}_\eta^2 = 0.0031$ and $\sigma_\zeta^2 = 0$, so that (3.60) reduces to (3.61), for which the slope was estimated as $\hat{\beta} = 0.0078$. Thus the trend component is a simple drifting random walk. The cycle variance was estimated as $\hat{\sigma}_\varepsilon^2 = 0.000013$, with a frequency of $\hat{\lambda}_c = 0.52\pi$, which implies a period of 3.8 months, while the damping factor was $\hat{\rho} = 0.94$. Since the implied amplitude of the cycle is only 0.4 per cent of the trend, such a cycle is clearly insignificant. The BSM therefore collapses to the model $y_t = \mu_t + \varepsilon_t$, with

$$\Delta\mu_t = 0.0078 + \eta_t$$
$$(0.0028)$$

and $\varepsilon_t \sim NID(0, 0.000013)$. Imposing the restriction that $\sigma_\varepsilon^2 = 0$ implies that y_t is itself a random walk with drift of 0.0078. However, a test of residual autocorrelation is significant, so that the BSM does not pick up the autoregressive structure found by the more traditional modelling of Example 3.2.

A BSM was also fitted to the annual UK output series analysed in Examples 2.2 and 2.6. Again σ_ζ^2 was found to be zero, leading to the estimated trend component

$$\Delta\mu_t = 0.0186 + \eta_t, \qquad \sigma_\eta^2 = 0.0005$$
$$(0.0019)$$

Here, though, $\hat{\lambda}_c = 0.16\pi$, implying a period of 12.4 years, $\hat{\rho} = 0.92$, and $\hat{\sigma}_\varepsilon^2 = 0.00017$. The estimated trend is superimposed on the observed series in Figure 3.10(a) and the cycle is shown in Figure

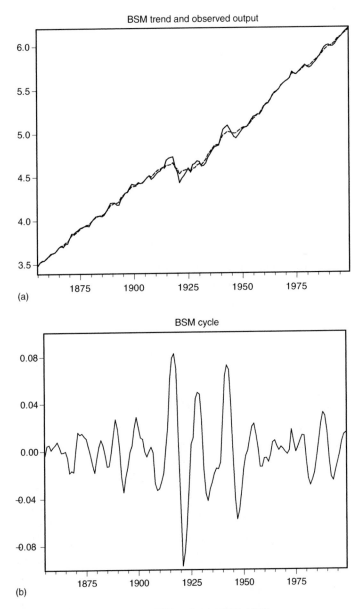

Figure 3.10   BSM components of UK output, 1855–1999

3.10(b). In comparison to the smooth transition trend and cycle shown in Figures 2.4 and 2.8, the BSM trend follows observed output much more closely and is therefore rather less smooth. Consequently, the cycle has a much smaller amplitude and is rather more smooth.

Further reading and background material

3.1 The classic reference to time series analysis is Box and Jenkins (1976). Detailed theoretical treatments of times series models are contained in many texts: Brockwell and Davis (1991), Hamilton (1994) and Gourieroux and Montfort (1997) are but a small selection. For more applied treatments, see, for example, Mills (1990, 1999). A formal treatment of difference and summation operators and lag polynomials may be found in Pollock (1999).

3.2 Formal methods of determining the correct degree of differencing of a time series are often referred to as *unit root* tests, for which there is an enormous literature. Maddala and Kim (1998) is a useful source of material with many references.

3.3 ARIMA modelling is sometimes referred to as 'Box–Jenkins' modelling, for obvious reasons. A major application of such models is in forecasting, which we do not explicitly consider here. As well as Box and Jenkins (1976), Granger and Newbold (1986) may usefully be consulted.

3.4 The TS–DS distinction is due to Nelson and Plosser (1982). Chan, Hayya and Ord (1977) and Nelson and Kang (1981, 1984) investigate the implications of incorrectly fitting a TS model to data generated by a DS process. The Dickey–Fuller critical values were originally published in Fuller (1976) (see also Dickey and Fuller, 1979) but are now automatically available in most econometric software packages. Critical values for segmented and smooth transition trend alternatives may be found in Perron (1989, 1997) and Leybourne, Newbold and Vougas (1998), respectively.

A more recent contribution to the research on the stochastic properties of US output mentioned in Example 3.4 is Murray and Nelson (2000).

3.5 The 'classic' UC model is due to Muth (1960), with Friedman (1957) containing a precursor model. The proof of the 'admissibility condition' is given by Lippi and Reichlin (1992). The B–N decomposition was developed by Beveridge and Nelson (1981), while the B–N smoother was proposed by Proietti and Harvey (2000). The method of computing the B–N decomposition used here is due to Cuddington and Winters (1987) and Miller (1988), while a more general approach is taken by Newbold (1990) and further extensions to $I(2)$ processes and seasonal models are provided by Newbold and Vougas (1996).

The classic reference on signal extraction is Whittle (1983), with Pierce (1979), Bell (1984) and Harvey and Koopman (2000) presenting many useful results. Structural models were popularised by Harvey (1985) and Harvey and Todd (1983). A thorough discussion of the methodological and technical ideas underlying such formulations and their estimation is contained in Harvey (1989) and Harvey and Shephard (1992), which also provide detailed accounts of the state space framework and the Kalman filter. Koopman *et al.* (2000) and Koopman, Shephard and Doornik (1999) provide computer software for state-space estimation of structural models, which are used to estimate the BSMs of Example 3.6.

4
Filtering Economic Time Series

4.1 Detrending using linear filters

4.1.1 Symmetric linear filters

In Chapter 2, section 2 we considered using moving averages to estimate a trend component. We now wish to take the analysis further and investigate the statistical implications of applying a moving average to an observed series. Thus, suppose we transform the observed series y_t to a new series y_t^* by using an MA $(2n + 1)$ filter

$$y_t^* = \Sigma_{j=-n}^n a_j y_{t-j} = a(B) y_t \tag{4.1}$$

where

$$a(B) = a_{-n} B^{-n} + a_{-n+1} B^{-n+1} + \ldots + a_0 + \ldots + a_{n-1} B^{n-1} + a_n B^n$$

is a two-sided linear filter. We now impose two conditions on $a(B)$: (i) that the filter weights sum to zero, $a(1) = \Sigma_{j=-n}^n a_j = 0$, and (ii) that the weights are symmetric, $a_j = a_{-j}$. Using these conditions, we can rewrite the filter as

$$a(B) = \Sigma_{j=-n}^n a_j B^j = \Sigma_{j=-n}^n \left(a_j B^j - a_j \right) = \Sigma_{j=1}^n a_j \left(B^j + B^{-j} - 2 \right)$$

Now, it is easy to demonstrate that

$$B^j + B^{-j} - 2 = -\left(1 - B^j\right)\left(1 - B^{-j}\right)$$

and

$$\left(1 - B^{\pm j}\right) = \left(1 - B^{\pm 1}\right)\left(1 + B^{\pm 1} + \ldots + B^{\pm(j-1)}\right)$$

so that

$$
\begin{aligned}
-\left(B^j + B^{-j} - 2\right) &= \left(1 - B\right)\left(1 - B^{-1}\right)\left(1 + B + \ldots + B^{j-1}\right)\left(1 + B^{-1} + \ldots + B^{-(j-1)}\right) \\
&= j + (j-1)\left(B + B^{-1}\right) + \ldots + 2\left(B^{j-2} + B^{-(j-2)}\right) \\
&\quad + \left(B^{j-1} + B^{-(j-1)}\right) \\
&= \Sigma_{h=-(j-1)}^{j-1}\left(j - |h|\right)B^h
\end{aligned}
$$

Thus

$$a(B) = -\Sigma_{j=1}^{n} a_j\left(1 - B^j\right)\left(1 - B^{-j}\right) = -\left(1 - B\right)\left(1 - B^{-1}\right)\Psi_n(B) \qquad (4.2)$$

where

$$\Psi_n(B) = \Sigma_{j=1}^{n} a_j\left(\Sigma_{h=-(j-1)}^{j-1}\left(j - |h|\right)B^h\right)$$

Since $\Psi_n(B)$ is a symmetric MA($2n - 1$) filter, it cannot alter the stationarity properties of any series to which it is applied. However, (4.2) shows that any symmetric filter $a(B)$ whose weights sum to zero contains the factor $(1 - B)(1 - B^{-1}) = -B + 2 - B^{-1}$, which will therefore render stationary not only $I(2)$ stochastic processes but also processes that contain quadratic deterministic trends. We can thus regard $a(B)$ as a 'trend elimination' filter, so that the corresponding 'trend extraction' filter is $b(B) = 1 - a(B)$, which has the same, but oppositely signed, weights as $a(B)$ except for the central value, $b_0 = 1 - a_0$, and hence $b(1) = 1$.

Example 4.1: The simple MA filter

Consider the simple MA($2n + 1$) filter

$$b(B) = \frac{1}{2n+1}\Sigma_{j=-n}^{n} B^j$$

which, as we know from Chapter 2, is a trend-extraction filter with $b(1) = 1$. The associated trend-elimination filter will then be

$$a(B) = 1 - b(B) = \frac{1}{2n+1}\Sigma_{j=-n}^{n} a_j B^j, \quad a_0 = 2n, \quad a_j = a_{-j} = -1, \quad j = 1,\ldots,n$$

with

$$\Psi_n(B) = -\frac{1}{2n+1}\Sigma_{j=1}^{n}\left(\Sigma_{h=-(j-1)}^{j-1}(j-|h|)B^h\right)$$

For $n = 3$, say, we have

$$\Psi_3(B) = -\frac{1}{7}\left(B^{-2} + 3B^{-1} + 6 + 3B + B^2\right)$$

and it can easily be checked that

$$-(1-B)(1-B^{-1})\Psi_3(B) = -\frac{1}{7}\left(-B^{-3} - B^{-2} - B^{-1} + 6 - B - B^2 - B^3\right) = a(B)$$

4.1.2 Frequency-domain properties of linear filters

It is useful here to develop some concepts from the frequency-domain perspective of time series analysis. Suppose that y_t, $t = 1, \ldots, T$, can be represented as the 'cyclical' process

$$y_t = \Sigma_{j=0}^{J}\left(\alpha_j \cos(\omega_j t) + \beta_j \sin(\omega_j t)\right) \tag{4.3}$$

where α_j and β_j are zero mean, i.i.d. random variables such that, for all j

$$E(\alpha_j^2) = E(\beta_j^2) = \sigma_j^2 \quad \text{and} \quad E(\alpha_j \beta_j) = 0$$

In (4.3), $\omega_j = 2\pi j/T$, so that $\omega_1 = 2\pi/T$ is the *fundamental frequency* and the jth sine and cosine functions complete j cycles every $T = 2\pi/\omega_j$ periods. (Note that setting $j = 0$ produces a 'constant' α_0, since $\cos(0) = 1$ and $\sin(0) = 0$.)

We may now make use of the two trigonometric identities

$$\cos(\omega_j t - \theta_j) = \cos\theta_j \cos(\omega_j t) + \sin\theta_j \sin(\omega_j t) \tag{4.4}$$

and

$$\cos(\omega_j t) \pm i\sin(\omega_j t) = \exp(\pm i\omega_j t) \tag{4.5}$$

where $i = \sqrt{-1}$. Using (4.4), (4.3) can be written

$$y_t = \Sigma_{j=1}^{J} \rho_j \cos(\omega_j t - \theta_j) \tag{4.6}$$

Since $\alpha_j = \rho_j \cos\theta_j$ and $\beta_j = \rho_j \sin\theta_j$, and using $\cos^2\theta_j + \sin^2\theta_j = 1$ and $\tan\theta_j = \sin\theta_j / \cos\theta_j$,

$$\rho_j^2 = \alpha_j^2 + \beta_j^2 \quad \text{and} \quad \theta_j = \tan^{-1}(\beta_j / \alpha_j).$$

In (4.6), $\rho_j \cos(\omega_j t - \theta_j)$ is known as the *j*th harmonic component of y_t. The *amplitude* (the distance from the peak to the trough of the cosine function) of this component is ρ_j, while its phase displacement, measured in radians, is θ_j. This delays, by θ_j / ω_j periods, the peak of the cosine function, which would occur, otherwise, at $t = 0$.

Using (4.5), known as the *Euler equations*, we have

$$\cos(\omega_j t) = \frac{1}{2}\big(\exp(i\omega_j t) + \exp(-i\omega_j t)\big)$$
$$\sin(\omega_j t) = -\frac{i}{2}\big(\exp(i\omega_j t) - \exp(-i\omega_j t)\big)$$

Equation (4.3) can then also be written as

$$y_t = \Sigma_{j=0}^{J} \left(\frac{\alpha_j - i\beta_j}{2}\exp(i\omega_j t) + \frac{\alpha_j + i\beta_j}{2}\exp(-i\omega_j t) \right)$$

or

$$y_t = \Sigma_{j=0}^{J} \big(\xi_j \exp(i\omega_j t) + \xi_j^* \exp(-i\omega_j t)\big) \tag{4.7}$$

where

$$\xi_j = (\alpha_j - i\beta_j)/2 \quad \text{and} \quad \xi_j^* = (\alpha_j + i\beta_j)/2$$

Thus, it follows that $E(y_t) = 0$ and $E(y_t^2) = \Sigma_{j=0}^{J} \sigma_j^2$, which is known as the *spectral decomposition* of the variance of y_t. The number of frequencies, J, depends upon the sample size, T. The highest frequency that can be detected when the series is observed at discrete time intervals is $\omega_J = \pi$, implying that $J = [T/2]$, where $[a]$ signifies the operation of taking the integer part of the argument a. π is termed the *Nyquist frequency*, being the highest frequency that can be detected from the observed data. For example, suppose the Jth component of y_t is a pure cosine wave of unit amplitude and zero phase ($\alpha_j = 1$, $\beta_j = 0$) with frequency lying in the interval $\pi < \omega_j < 2\pi$. If we let $\omega_j^* = 2\pi - \omega_j$, then

$$\begin{aligned}\cos(\omega_j t) &= \cos\left((2\pi - \omega_j^*)t\right) \\ &= \cos(2\pi)\cos(\omega_j^* t) + \sin(2\pi)\sin(\omega_j^* t) \\ &= \cos(\omega_j^* t)\end{aligned}$$

where we use the identities $\cos(A - B) = \cos A \cos B + \sin A \sin B$, $\cos(2\pi) = 1$ and $\sin(2\pi) = 0$. Hence ω_j is indistinguishable from ω_j^*, the latter being known as the *alias* of the former.

With these preliminaries, we are now in a position to define the spectral representation of the *infinite* sequence y_t, which is the continuous counterpart of (4.7) when both $T \to \infty$ and $J \to \infty$:

$$y_t = \int_0^\pi \left(e^{i\omega t}dZ(\omega) + e^{-i\omega t}dZ^*(\omega)\right) = \int_{-\pi}^\pi e^{i\omega t}dZ(\omega) \tag{4.8}$$

$dZ(\omega)$ and $dZ^*(\omega)$ are complex stochastic processes obtained in the following way. We first define $\alpha_j = dA(\omega_j)$ and $\beta_j = dB(\omega_j)$, where $A(\omega)$ and $B(\omega)$ are step functions with discontinuities at ω_j, $j = 0, \ldots, J$, and write these as $dA(\omega)$ and $dB(\omega)$ in the limit as $J \to \infty$. $dZ(\omega)$ and $dZ^*(\omega)$ can then be defined analogously to ξ_j and ξ_j^* in (4.7) as

$$dZ(\omega) = \frac{\left(dA(\omega) - idB(\omega)\right)}{2} \quad \text{and} \quad dZ^*(\omega) = \frac{\left(dA(\omega) + idB(\omega)\right)}{2}$$

The $dA(\omega)$ and $dB(\omega)$ are assumed to be zero mean i.i.d. stochastic processes that are mutually uncorrelated, so that

$$\begin{aligned} E\left(dA(\omega)dB(\lambda)\right) &= 0 \quad \text{for all } \omega, \lambda \\ E\left(dA(\omega)dA(\lambda)\right) &= 0 \quad \text{if } \omega \neq \lambda \\ E\left(dB(\omega)dB(\lambda)\right) &= 0 \quad \text{if } \omega \neq \lambda \end{aligned}$$

and

$$E\big(dA(\omega)\big)^2 = E\big(dB(\omega)\big)^2 = 2dF(\omega) = 2f(\omega)d\omega$$

From these conditions, it follows that

$$E\big(dZ(\omega)dZ^*(\lambda)\big) = 0 \qquad \text{if } \omega \neq \lambda$$
$$E\big(dZ(\omega)dZ^*(\omega)\big) = dF(\omega)$$

$F(\omega)$ is the *spectral distribution function* and its derivative, $f(\omega) = dF(\omega)/d\omega$, is the *spectral density function*.

The second equality in (4.8) results from regarding $A(\omega)$ as an even function, such that $A(-\omega) = A(\omega)$, and $B(\omega)$ as an odd function such that $B(-\omega) = -B(\omega)$, thus implying that $dZ^*(\omega) = dZ(-\omega)$.

Consider now the spectral representation of the filter (4.1):

$$
\begin{aligned}
y_t^* = \Sigma_j a_j y_{t-j} &= \Sigma_j a_j \left(\int_\omega e^{i\omega(t-j)} dZ(\omega) \right) \\
&= \int_\omega e^{i\omega t} \left(\Sigma_j a_j e^{-i\omega j} \right) dZ(\omega) \qquad (4.9) \\
&= \int_\omega a(\omega) e^{i\omega t} dZ(\omega) = \int_\omega e^{i\omega t} dZ_\alpha(\omega)
\end{aligned}
$$

where $dZ_a(\omega) = a(\omega)dZ(\omega)$, with $a(\omega) = \Sigma_j a_j e^{-i\omega j}$ being termed the *frequency response function*. The spectral density of y_t^* is then

$$
\begin{aligned}
f_a(\omega)d\omega = E\big(dZ_a(\omega)dZ_a^*(\omega)\big) &= E\big(dZ_a(\omega)dZ_a(-\omega)\big) \\
&= a(\omega)a(-\omega)E\big(dZ(\omega)dZ^*(\omega)\big) \\
&= |a(\omega)|^2 E\big(dZ(\omega)dZ^*(\omega)\big) \\
&= |a(\omega)|^2 f(\omega)d\omega
\end{aligned}
$$

Since we can write

$$a(\omega) = \Sigma_j a_j \cos(\omega j) - i\Sigma_j a_j \sin(\omega j)$$

it follows that

$$|a(\omega)|^2 = \left(\Sigma_j a_j \cos(\omega j) \right)^2 + \left(\Sigma_j a_j \sin(\omega j) \right)^2$$

and

$$a(\omega) = |a(\omega)| \exp(-i\theta(\omega)) \qquad (4.10)$$

where

$$\theta(\omega) = \tan^{-1} \frac{\Sigma_j a_j \sin(\omega j)}{\Sigma_j a_j \cos(\omega j)}$$

The function $|a(\omega)|$ is called the *gain* of the filter and indicates the extent to which the amplitude of the cyclical components of y_t are altered through the filtering operation. $|a(\omega)|^2$ is known as the *power transfer* function. $\theta(\omega)$ is the *phase shift* and indicates the extent to which the cyclical components are displaced in time. If $a(\omega)$ is symmetric, $a(\omega) = a(-\omega)$, so that $a(\omega) = |a(\omega)|$ and, from (4.10), $\theta(\omega) = 0$, which is the condition for *phase neutrality*.

Substituting (4.10) into (4.9) gives

$$y_t^* = \int_{-\pi}^{\pi} \exp(i(\omega t - \theta(\omega)))|a(\omega)|dZ(\omega)$$
$$= \int_{-\pi}^{\pi} \exp(i\omega(t - \theta(\omega)/\omega))|a(\omega)|dZ(\omega)$$

which summarises the two effects of the filter. Note that the condition that the filter weights sum to zero implies that the frequency response function, and hence the gain, is zero at $\omega = 0$: $a(0) = \Sigma_j a_j e^{-i0j} = 0$ only if $\Sigma_j a_j = 0$

Example 4.2: The gain and phase of the simple MA and first differencing filters

The simple MA $(2n + 1)$ filter of Example 4.1 has frequency response function

$$a(\omega) = \frac{1}{2n+1} \Sigma_{j=-n}^{n} e^{-i\omega j}$$

We may now use the result that

$$\Sigma_{j=-n}^{n} e^{-i\omega j} = e^{-in\omega}\left(1 + e^{i\omega} + e^{i2\omega} + \ldots + e^{i2n\omega}\right)$$
$$= e^{-in\omega} \frac{1 - e^{i(2n+1)\omega}}{1 - e^{i\omega}} = \frac{e^{-in\omega} - e^{i(n+1)\omega}}{1 - e^{i\omega}}$$

Multiplying both the numerator and the denominator of this expression by $-e^{-i\omega 2}$ yields

$$\frac{-e^{-i\omega 2}\left(e^{-in\omega} - e^{i(n+1)\omega}\right)}{-e^{-i\omega 2}\left(1 - e^{-i\omega}\right)} = \frac{e^{i(2n+1)\omega/2} - e^{-i(2n+1)\omega/2}}{e^{i\omega 2}e^{-i\omega/2}} = \frac{\sin((2n+1)\omega/2)}{\sin(\omega/2)}$$

so that

$$a(\omega) = \frac{\sin\big((2n+1)\omega/2\big)}{(2n+1)\sin(\omega/2)} \tag{4.11}$$

Since $a(\omega)$ is real, reflecting the symmetry of the filter, the gain is given by the absolute value of (4.11). Since the filter is symmetric, the phase displacement is zero. The gain is shown graphically in Figure 4.1(a) for $n = 2$. This shows that the filtered series will be smoother than the original, since the gain at high frequencies is relatively small, so that irregular movements in the original are damped. In addition, the gain is zero at the fundamental frequency, $\omega = 2\pi/5$, and at the harmonic, $4\pi/5$.

Consider now the first difference 'filter' $y_t^* = y_t - y_{t-1}$ with frequency response function $a(\omega) = 1 - e^{-i\omega}$. The power transfer function of this filter is

$$|a(\omega)|^2 = |1 - e^{-i\omega}|^2 = \big(1 - e^{-i\omega}\big)\big(1 - e^{-i\omega}\big) = 2 - \big(e^{i\omega} + e^{-i\omega}\big) = 2 - 2\cos(\omega)$$

The graph of the gain $|a(\omega)| = 2^{1/2}(1-\cos(\omega))^{1/2}$ is shown in Figure 4.1(b) and shows that it is zero at $\omega = 0$ and that there is no smoothing at high frequencies. Indeed, higher frequencies are given more weight, so that short-term fluctuations are emphasised at the expense of long-run components. Since the filter is asymmetric, it induces a phase shift of $\theta(\omega) = \tan^{-1}(-\sin(\omega)/(1 - \cos(\omega)))$.

Example 4.3: Spurious cyclical behaviour

Suppose two filters, $a_1(B)$ and $a_2(B)$, are applied consecutively, so that

$$y_t^* = a_1(B)a_2(B)y_t = a(B)y_t$$

The frequency response function is thus $a(\omega) = a_1(\omega)a_2(\omega)$, with power transfer function $|a_1(\omega)|^2|a_2(\omega)|^2$. The extension to applying several filters consecutively is immediate. Consider then the filter produced by differencing y_t d times,

$$a_d(\omega) = (1 - e^{-i\omega})^d$$

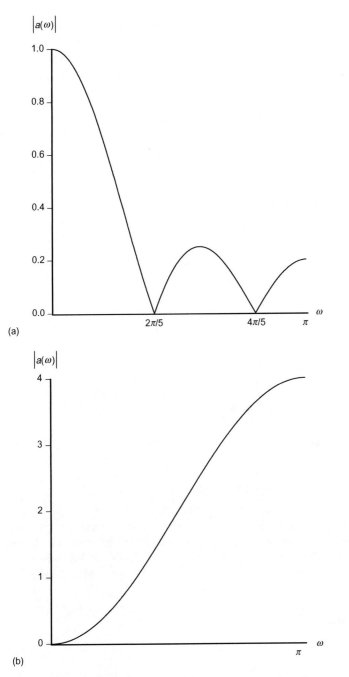

(a)

(b)

Figure 4.1 Gain functions for (a) MA(5) filter, and (b) first difference filter

to which we then apply the summation filter $1 + B$ s times, i.e.

$$a_s(\omega) = (1 + e^{-i\omega})^s$$

The resultant series, $y_t^* = (1 - B)^d(1 + B)^s y_t$, will then have the power transfer function

$$|a(\omega)|^2 = 2^{d+s}(1 - \cos(\omega))^d (1 + \cos(\omega))^s \tag{4.12}$$

As the differencing operations attenuate the low frequencies, while the summations attenuate the high frequencies, the combined effect will be to emphasise certain of the intermediate frequencies, which will reveal itself as a peak in the transfer function. Differentiating (4.12) with respect to ω and setting the result to zero yields

$$d(1 + \cos(\omega)) - s(1 - \cos(\omega)) = 0$$

i.e.

$$\omega_0 = \cos^{-1} \frac{s - d}{s + d}$$

is the peak frequency. Here we make use of $\partial \cos(\omega)/\partial(\omega) = -\sin(\omega)$ and taking the second derivative confirms that ω_0 is indeed a maximum. By suitable choices of d and s, ω_0 can be made arbitrarily close to any frequency that we like, and the larger d and s are, the sharper is the peak of the transfer function. Figure 4.2 shows transfer functions for $d = 10$, $s = 2$ and $d = 4$, $s = 8$, in which these features, known as the *Slutsky effect*, are clearly shown.

4.1.3 Designing a low-pass filter

Given these properties of linear filters, we are now in a position to design an optimal filter, in the sense that it emphasises specified frequency bands. A basic building block in filter design is the *low-pass* filter, which is a filter that retains only slow-moving, low-frequency, components of a time series. An ideal low-pass filter, which we denote $a_L(\omega)$, passes only frequencies in the interval $-\omega_c < \omega < \omega_c$, where ω_c is the *cut-off* frequency. It therefore has the frequency response function

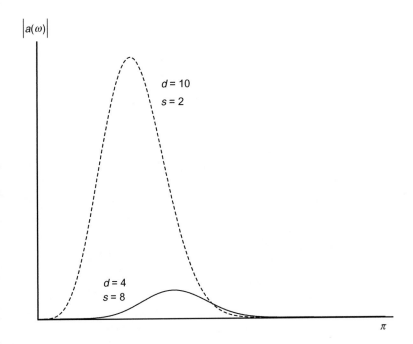

Figure 4.2   Examples of the Slutsky effect

$$a_L(\omega) = \begin{cases} 1 & \text{if } \omega < |\omega_c| \\ 0 & \text{if } \omega \geq |\omega_c| \end{cases} \tag{4.13}$$

The filter should also be phase-neutral, so that temporal shifts are not induced by filtering, and it should also have trend-elimination properties. Thus we also require that $a_L(\omega) = a_L(-\omega)$ and $a_L(0) = 0$, and these are guaranteed if the filter weights are symmetric and sum to zero, as assumed in subsection 4.1.2 above.

Since the frequency response function is

$$a_L(\omega) = \sum_{j=-\infty}^{\infty} a_{L,j} e^{-i\omega j}$$

the filter weights are given by the 'inverse'

$$a_{L,j} = \frac{1}{2\pi} \int_{-\pi}^{\pi} a_L(\omega) e^{i\omega j} d\omega = \frac{1}{2\pi} \int_{-\omega_c}^{\omega_c} e^{i\omega j} d\omega$$

where the second equality follows from (4.13). Thus

$$a_{L,0} = \frac{1}{2\pi} \int_{-\omega_c}^{\omega_c} d\omega = \frac{\omega_c}{\pi}$$

and

$$a_{L,j} = \frac{1}{2\pi} \left[\frac{e^{i\omega j}}{ij} \right]_{-\omega_c}^{\omega_c} = \frac{1}{\pi j} \sin(\omega_c j), \quad j \neq 0$$

which uses the result from the Euler equations (4.5) that $2i\sin(\omega_c j) = \exp(i\omega_c j) - \exp(-i\omega_c j)$.

Although the weights $a_{L,j}$ tend to zero as j becomes large, an infinite-order moving average is needed to construct an ideal filter. In practice, we must approximate an ideal filter with a finite moving average of the form (4.1), with frequency response function

$$a_{L,n}(\omega) = \Sigma_{j=-n}^{n} a_j e^{-i\omega j}$$

rather than $a_l(\omega)$. A natural approximation strategy is to choose the approximating filter's weights to minimise

$$Q = \frac{1}{2\pi} \int_{-\pi}^{\pi} |a_L(\omega) - a_{L,n}(\omega)|^2 d\omega$$

subject to the restriction that $a_{L,n}(0) = \Sigma_{j=-n}^{n} a_j = \phi$, say, where ϕ is typically zero or unity. The Lagrangean for this problem is $\ell = -Q + 2\lambda_n (a_{L,n}(0) - \phi)$, which may be expressed as

$$\ell = -\frac{1}{2\pi} \int_{-\pi}^{\pi} \left(a_L(\omega) - \Sigma_{j=-n}^{n} a_n e^{-i\omega n} \right) \left(a_L(\omega) - \Sigma_{j=-n}^{n} a_n e^{-i\omega n} \right)' d\omega$$
$$+ 2\lambda_n \left(\Sigma_{j=-n}^{n} a_j - \phi \right)$$

The first-order condition for a_j is

$$0 = \frac{1}{2\pi} \int_{-\pi}^{\pi} e^{-i\omega j} \left(a_L(\omega) - \Sigma_{j=-n}^{n} a_n e^{-i\omega n} \right)' d\omega$$
$$+ \frac{1}{2\pi} \int_{-\pi}^{\pi} e^{i\omega j} \left(a_L(\omega) - \Sigma_{j=-n}^{n} a_n e^{-i\omega n} \right) d\omega + 2\lambda_n$$

A useful result at this point is

$$\frac{1}{2\pi}\int_{-\pi}^{\pi} e^{-i\omega(j-k)}d\omega = \begin{cases} 1 & \text{for } j = k \\ 0 & \text{for } j \neq k \end{cases} \tag{4.14}$$

Repeatedly applying (4.14), the first-order condition for a_j can be expressed as

$$0 = (a_{L,j} - a_j) + \lambda_n \tag{4.15}$$

Summing the conditions (4.15) yields

$$\Sigma_{j=-n}^{n} a_j = \phi = \Sigma_{j=-n}^{a} a_{L,n} - (2n+1)\lambda_n$$

so that

$$\lambda_n = \frac{\phi - \Sigma_{j=-n}^{n} a_{L,n}}{2n+1}$$

and

$$a_j = \begin{cases} a_{L,j} - \lambda_n, & |j| \leq n \\ 0 & j > n \end{cases}$$

If there is no constraint on $a_{L,n}(0)$, so that $\lambda_n = 0$, then it follows that the optimal approximation sets $a_j = a_{L,j}$ for $j = 0, 1, \ldots, n$ and $a_j = 0$ for $j > n$, so that the optimal approximate filter simply involves truncation of the ideal filter's weights.

4.1.4 High-pass and band-pass filters

The low-pass filter defined above removes high-frequency components while retaining low-frequency components. A high-pass filter does the reverse, so that the complementary high-pass filter to (4.13) has weights $a_{H,0} = 1 - a_{L,0}$ at $j = 0$ and $a_{H,j} = -a_{L,j}$ at $j \neq 0$.

The ideal band-pass filter passes only frequencies in the ranges $\omega_{L1} \leq |\omega| \leq \omega_{L2}$, so that it can be constructed as the difference between two low-pass filters with cut-off frequencies ω_{L1} and ω_{L2}. It's frequency response function will therefore be $a_B(\omega) = a_{L2}(\omega) - a_{L1}(\omega)$, where $a_{L2}(\omega)$ and $a_{L1}(\omega)$ are the frequency response functions of the two low-pass filters, since this will give a frequency response of unity in the band $\omega_{L1} \leq |\omega| \leq \omega_{L2}$ and zero elsewhere. It is thus clear that the weights of the band-pass filter will be given by $a_{B,j} = a_{L2,j} - a_{L1,j}$, where $a_{L2,j}$ and $a_{L1,j}$ are the weights of the two low-pass filters.

Having defined these types of filters in terms of frequencies, it is often useful to work with *periodicities*. Thus a cycle of frequency ω will have a periodicity of $2\pi/\omega$ time periods (or, equivalently, $\omega/2\pi$ cycles will be traversed each period). Thus an approximate low-pass filter that is truncated at lag n, and which passes components with periodicity greater than or equal to $p = 2\pi/\omega_c$, will be denoted $LP_n(p)$. Since the ideal filter has $n = \infty$, this can be denoted $LP_\infty(p)$. Similarly, we may define the complementary high-pass filter $HP_n(p) = 1 - LP_n(p)$ and the approximate band-pass filter that passes cycles between p and $q(>p)$ periods in length as $BP_n(p, q) = LP_n(p) - LP_n(q)$.

The choice of n is fundamental to the quality of the approximation to the ideal filter. If n is set too small, approximate filters will suffer from *leakage, compression* and *exacerbation*. Taking a high-pass filter for illustration, leakage is the phenomenon whereby the filter passes through frequencies that it was designed to suppress, including them with those the filter was designed to retain. This manifests itself in the tendency for the filter to have nonzero frequency response for frequencies below the cut-off. *Compression* refers to the tendency for a filter to have less than unit frequency response for frequencies just above the cut-off, while *exacerbation* describes the situation when the frequency response is in excess of unity. As frequencies get longer, the frequency response function of the filter has a tendency to oscillate between compression and exacerbation, which is typically referred to as the *Gibbs phenomenon*. These features are seen in Figure 4.3, which shows an ideal high-pass filter (constrained to have $a_H(1) = 1$) with $p = 32$, so that the cut-off frequency is $\omega_c = \pi/16$, or 0.03 cycles per period. Superimposed on this ideal filter are approximate high-pass filters with $n = 4, 8, 12$ and 16. When $n = 4$ there are major departures from the ideal filter, with the approximating filter displaying excessive leakage and a pronounced Gibbs phenomenon. Leakage is reduced as n increases but, interestingly, the Gibbs phenomenon does not disappear: it is almost as pronounced for $n = 16$ as it is for $n = 12$. This suggests that an optimal setting of n is not possible, particularly as increasing n leads to more 'lost' observations at the beginning and end of the filtered series.

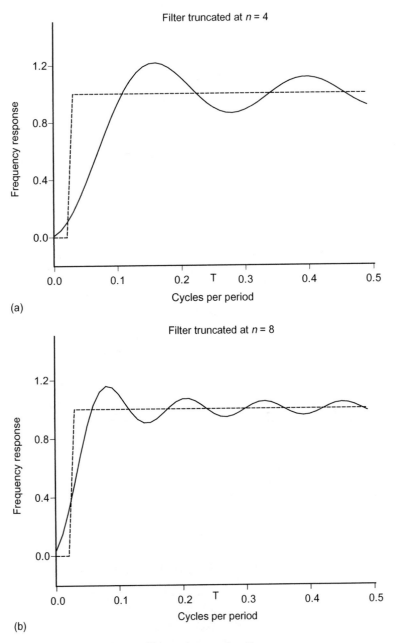

Figure 4.3 Ideal high-pass filter and approximations

90

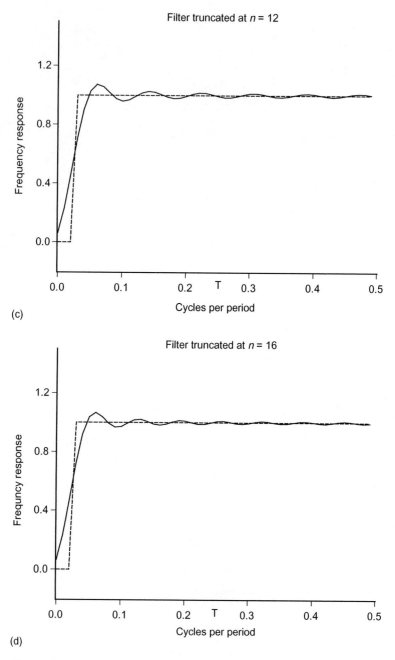

Figure 4.3 (*continued*)

Example 4.4: Band-pass business cycle filters

A conventional definition of the business cycle emphasises fluctuations of between 6 and 32 quarters. Assuming that y_t is observed quarterly, then a band-pass filter that passes only frequencies corresponding to these periods, i.e., $\omega_{L1} = \pi/16$ and $\omega_{L2} = \pi/3$, is given by the $BP_n(6, 32)$ filter $y_t^* = a_B(B)y_t$, whose weights are defined as

$$a_{B,0} = a_{L2,0} - a_{L1,0} = \frac{1}{3} - \frac{1}{16} - \left(\lambda_{L2,n} - \lambda_{L1,n}\right)$$

$$a_{B,j} = a_{L2,j} - a_{L1,j} = \frac{1}{\pi j}\left(\sin\left(\frac{\pi j}{3}\right) - \sin\left(\frac{\pi j}{16}\right)\right) - \left(\lambda_{L2,n} - \lambda_{L1,n}\right), \quad j \neq 0$$

where

$$\lambda_{L2,n} = -\frac{\sum_{j=-n}^{n} a_{L2,n}}{2n+1}, \quad \lambda_{L1,n} = -\frac{\sum_{j=-n}^{n} a_{L1,n}}{2n+1}$$

since $\phi = 0$ because $a_B(B)$ is a trend-elimination filter.

Setting $n = 12$ has been found to be a useful compromise between mitigating the impact of leakage and compression and minimising the loss of filtered observations, and this yields the set of filter weights given in column (1) of Table 4.1, which may be used if quarterly observations are available on y_t. If only annual data are available, then the $BP_3(2, 8)$ filter is appropriate, whose weights are given in column (3) of Table 4.1.

Table 4.1 Moving average weights for band-pass business cycle filters

j (1)	BP_{12} (6, 32) (2)	BP_3 (2, 8) (3)
0	0.2777	0.7741
1	0.2204	−0.2010
2	0.0838	−0.1351
3	−0.0521	−0.0510
4	−0.1184	
5	−0.1012	
6	−0.0422	
7	0.0016	
8	0.0015	
9	−0.0279	
10	−0.0501	
11	−0.0423	
12	−0.0119	

4.2   The Hodrick–Prescott filter

4.2.1   The Hodrick–Prescott filter in infinite samples

A popular technique for extracting a cyclical component is the *Hodrick–Prescott* filter. This was originally developed as the solution to the problem of minimising the variation in the cyclical component of an observed time series, $\varepsilon_t = y_t - \mu_t$, subject to a condition on the 'smoothness' of the trend component, μ_t. This smoothness condition penalises acceleration in the trend, so that the minimisation problem becomes that of minimising

$$\sum_{t=1}^{T} \varepsilon_t^2 + \lambda \sum_{t=1}^{T} \left[(\mu_{t+1} - \mu_t) - (\mu_t - \mu_{t-1}) \right]^2$$

with respect to μ_t, $t = 0, 1, \ldots, T + 1$, and where λ is a Lagrangean multiplier that can be interpreted as a smoothness parameter. The higher the value of λ, the smoother is the trend, so that in the limit, as $\lambda \to \infty$, μ_t becomes a linear trend. The first-order conditions are

$$\begin{aligned}
0 = {}& -2(y_t - \mu_t) + 2\lambda \left[(\mu_t - \mu_{t-1}) - (\mu_{t-1} - \mu_{t-2}) \right] \\
& - 4\lambda \left[(\mu_{t+1} - \mu_t) - (\mu_t - \mu_{t-1}) \right] \\
& + 2\lambda \left[(\mu_{t+2} - \mu_{t+1}) - (\mu_{t+1} - \mu_t) \right]
\end{aligned}$$

which may be written as

$$y_t = \mu_t + \lambda(1 - B)^2 (\mu_t - 2\mu_{t+1} + \mu_{t+2}) = \left(1 + \lambda(1 - B)^2(1 - B^{-1})^2 \right)\mu_t \tag{4.16}$$

We will denote the Hodrick–Prescott filter as $H\text{–}P[(\lambda)]$ to distinguish it from the high-pass filter $HP_n(p)$ introduced earlier. The *H–P* trend extraction filter is thus given by

$$b_{H-P}(B) = \left(1 + \lambda(1 - B)^2(1 - B^{-1})^2 \right)^{-1}$$

and the trend-elimination, or *H–P* cycle, filter is

$$a_{H-P}(B) = 1 - b_{H-P}(B) = \frac{\lambda(1 - B)^2(1 - B^{-1})^2}{1 + \lambda(1 - B)^2(1 - B^{-1})^2} = \frac{\lambda B^{-2}\Delta^4}{1 + \lambda B^{-2}\Delta^4} \tag{4.17}$$

which thus has the frequency response function

$$a_{H-P}(\omega) = \frac{\lambda(1-e^{-i\omega})^2(1-e^{i\omega})^2}{1+\lambda(1-e^{-i\omega})^2(1-e^{i\omega})^2} = \frac{4\lambda(1-\cos(\omega))^2}{1+4\lambda(1-\cos(\omega))^2}$$

$$= \frac{4(1-\cos(\omega))^2}{\lambda^{-1}+4(1-\cos(\omega))^2}$$

The *H–P* cycle filter shares several important properties with an ideal high-pass filter. It has zero gain at $\omega = 0$ since $|a_{H-P}(0)|$ is clearly zero; it will also render stationary $I(4)$ processes, since (4.17) contains the factor Δ^4 in the numerator; and it is symmetric, so that there is no phase shift. Figure 4.4 shows the frequency response function of the *H–P*(1600) filter superimposed upon the ideal high-pass $HP_\infty(32)$ filter and confirms that the former is a close approximation to the latter.

Note also that the *H–P* filter shows no 'Gibbs phenomenon' in that the frequency response function does not oscillate around

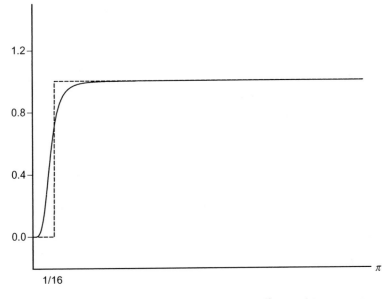

Figure 4.4   Frequency response of the *H–P* filter with smoothing parameter $\lambda = 1,600$ and ideal high-pass filter for $p = 32$

unity as ω increases. This would seem to imply that the *H–P* filter should be preferred to an approximate high-pass filter of the type shown in Figure 4.3.

4.2.2   The finite sample H–P filter

Figure 4.4 shows the 'ideal' *H–P*(1600) frequency response in that we have implicitly assumed that the filter is applied to a series of infinite length, since the rational form of the filter in (4.17) implies that $a_{H-P}(B)$ is a two-sided infinite moving average. With finite samples, one obvious strategy to adopt is to truncate the weights at some fixed lag, analogous to the approximation of the ideal filters discussed above. In practice, however, an alternative procedure is typically used, which has the apparently attractive feature of involving no loss of data at the ends of the series. The finite sample *H–P*(λ) filter is based on (4.16), which can be written as

$$y_t = \lambda\mu_{t-2} - 4\lambda\mu_{t-1} + (1+6\lambda)\mu_t - 4\lambda\mu_{t+1} + \lambda\mu_{t+2}$$

so that

$$\varepsilon_t = y_t - \mu_t = \lambda(\mu_{t-2} - 4\mu_{t-1} + 6\mu_t - 4\mu_{t+1} + \mu_{t+2})$$

Note that this expression cannot be used when $t = 1, 2, T - 1$ and T. At the end points of the sample, the expression is modified to

$$\varepsilon_t = \lambda(\mu_1 - 2\mu_2 + \mu_3)$$
$$\varepsilon_t = \lambda(-2\mu_1 + 5\mu_2 - 4\mu_3 + \mu_4)$$
$$\varepsilon_{T-1} = \lambda(\mu_{T-3} - 4\mu_{T-2} + 5\mu_{T-1} - 2\mu_T)$$
$$\varepsilon_T = \lambda(\mu_{T-2} - 2\mu_{T-1} + \mu_T)$$

Defining $\mathbf{y} = (y_1, ..., y_T)'$, $\boldsymbol{\mu} = (\mu_1, ..., \mu_T)'$, $\boldsymbol{\varepsilon} = (\varepsilon_1, ..., \varepsilon_T)'$, $\mathbf{y} - \boldsymbol{\mu}$, and

$$
\Gamma = \begin{bmatrix}
1 & -2 & 1 & 0 & 0 & 0 & 0 & & \cdots & & 0 \\
-2 & 5 & -4 & 1 & 0 & 0 & 0 & & \cdots & & 0 \\
1 & -4 & 6 & -4 & 1 & 0 & 0 & & \cdots & & 0 \\
0 & 1 & -4 & 6 & -4 & 1 & 0 & & \cdots & & 0 \\
\vdots & & & & & & & & & & \vdots \\
0 & & \cdots & & & 0 & 1 & -4 & 6 & -4 & 1 & 0 \\
0 & & \cdots & & & 0 & 0 & 1 & -4 & 6 & -4 & 1 \\
0 & & \cdots & & & 0 & 0 & 0 & 1 & -4 & 5 & -2 \\
0 & & \cdots & & & 0 & 0 & 0 & 0 & 1 & -2 & 1
\end{bmatrix}
$$

the 'system' can be written as $\varepsilon = \lambda\Gamma\mu$. Replacing μ by $y - \varepsilon$ yields the vector of cyclical components $\varepsilon = (I + \lambda\Gamma)^{-1}\lambda\Gamma y$. The non-symmetric nature of the Γ matrix induces a phase shift near the end points of the data, as well as gains that differ sharply between observations and from the ideal filter. As we move closer to the centre of the data, these phase shifts disappear and the gains become more similar. Consequently, the finite sample *H–P* filter does not really generate useful estimates of the cyclical component at the ends of the sample.

4.2.3 Optimising the smoothing parameter

As we have seen in Figure 4.4, setting the smoothing parameter to $\lambda = 1,600$ produces a frequency response function that is very close to that of the ideal high-pass filter with $p = 32$, i.e., if quarterly data is being used, then this choice produces a filter that is close to the optimal for passing cyclical components having periods of 32 quarters or less, which corresponds to conventional views of the business cycle. Two questions arise from such a statement: first, are there better choices for λ when using quarterly data and, second, what values should be chosen for annual or monthly data? This has generated a good deal of research and recent evidence suggests that, when filtering quarterly data with a near unit root, the optimal value of the smoothing parameter lies in the range 1000–1050, although the standard value of $\lambda = 1,600$ does not lead to serious distortions. For annual data, a much smaller value for λ should be selected, between 5 and 10, while for monthly data much larger values should be chosen, these being in the region of 80,000 to 160,000.

Example 4.5: Band-pass and Hodrick–Prescott cycles for US output

Figure 4.5 shows band-pass and *H–P* cycles for the US quarterly output series. The band-pass cycle is calculated as $BP_{12}(6, 32)$ and hence uses the weights shown in Table 4.1, thus losing three years worth of data at the start and end of the sample. The smoothing parameter for the *H–P* cycle is chosen to be $\lambda = 1,000$. Because the *H–P* cycle is effectively a high-pass filter with $p = 32$, it basically differs from the band-pass cycle in admitting high-frequency components that the latter filters out. This manifests itself in a less smooth cycle, although the overall pattern of fluctuations is almost identical.

96

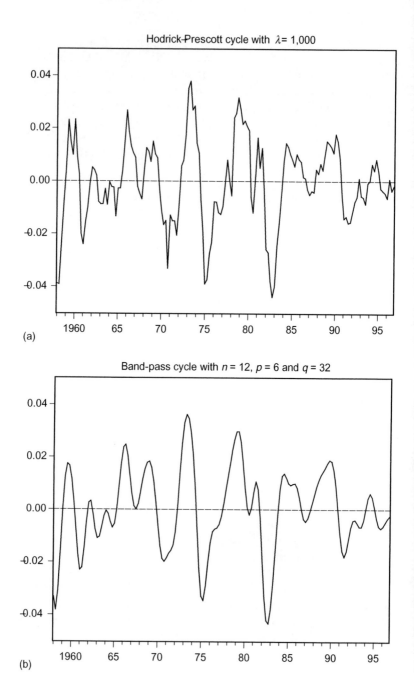

Figure 4.5 Hodrick–Prescott and band-pass cycles for US output

Example 4.6: H–P filtering of UK output

Figure 4.6(a) shows the annual UK output series with the *H–P*(10) trend extraction filter superimposed, while Figure 4.6(b) plots the associated cycle, with the cycle obtained from the segmented trend model of Example 2.6 also shown for comparison. The *H–P* trend 'smooths out' the rapid transition in 1919 and 1920, with the result that the cyclical component is much larger and more volatile during the early 1920s. In contrast, the *H–P* cycle is smaller during the Second World War and throughout the period from 1950 to 1980, since the *H–P* trend responds to current data in this period, rather than being restricted to a linear function of time as in the segmented trend model.

4.3   Filters and structural models

4.3.1   A structural model for the H–P filter

Recall the UC model analysed in Chapter 3, section 3.5, written here as

$$\Delta \mu_t = \gamma(B)v_t$$

and

$$\varepsilon_t = \delta(B)u_t,$$

so that

$$\Delta y_t = \gamma(B)v_t + \Delta \delta(B)u_t = \theta(B)e_t$$

where

$$\sigma_e^2 \theta(B)\theta(B^{-1}) = \sigma_v^2 \gamma(B)\gamma(B^{-1}) + \sigma_u^2(1-B)(1-B^{-1})\delta(B)\delta(B^{-1})$$

The WK filter estimate of μ_t is given by

$$\mu_{t|T} = \frac{\sigma_v^2 \gamma(B)\gamma(B^{-1})}{\sigma_e^2 \theta(B)\theta(B^{-1})} y_t$$

$$= \frac{\gamma(B)\gamma(B^{-1})}{\gamma(B)\gamma(B^{-1}) + (\sigma_u^2/\sigma_v^2)(1-B)(1-B^{-1})\delta(B)\delta(B^{-1})} y_t$$

(4.18)

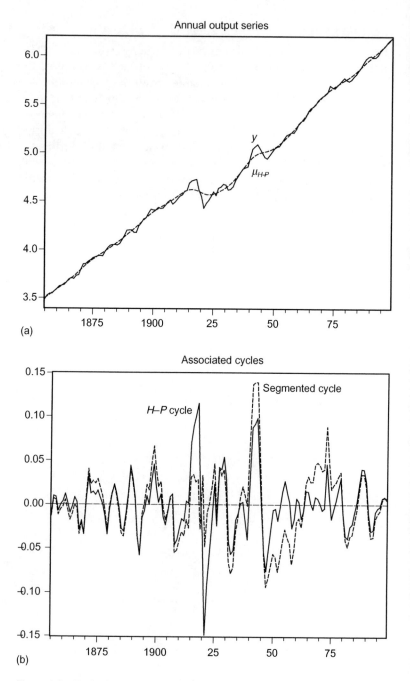

(a)

(b)

Figure 4.6 Hodrick–Prescott trend and cycle ($\lambda = 10$) for UK output

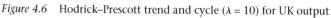

Comparing the filter in (4.18) with the H–P trend-extraction filter

$$b_{H-P}(B) = \left(1 + \lambda(1 - B)^2(1 - B^{-1})^2\right)^{-1}$$

shows that, for the latter to be an optimal filter in the WK sense, we must set

$$\gamma(B) = (1 - B)^{-1}, \quad \delta(B) = 1, \quad \lambda = \sigma_u^2 / \sigma_v^2$$

In other words, the underlying UC model must have the trend component

$$\Delta^2 \mu_t = v_t$$

which is, in effect, the 'smooth trend' model (3.62), and a *white noise* cyclical component, since $\varepsilon_t = u_t$. The frequency response function of the *H–P* estimate of this component is shown in Figure 4.4 and is certainly not that of white noise.

4.3.2 The Butterworth filter

Consider now an alternative UC model taking the form

$$\Delta^d \mu_t = (1 + B)^n v_t$$

and

$$\varepsilon_t = (1 - B)^{n-d} u_t$$

This has the WK trend filter estimate $\hat{\mu}_t = \psi_T(B)y_t$, where

$$\psi_T(B) = \frac{(1 + B)^n(1 + B^{-1})^n}{(1 + B)^n(1 + B^{-1})^n + \lambda(1 - B)^n(1 - B^{-1})^n} \tag{4.19}$$

$\psi_T(B)$ is known as the *Butterworth square-wave filter*. The optimal estimate of the cycle is then

$$\hat{\varepsilon}_t = y_t - \hat{\mu}_t = \left(1 - \psi_T(B)\right)y_t = \psi_C(B)y_t$$

so that

$$\psi_C(B) = \frac{\lambda(1 - B)^n(1 - B^{-1})^n}{(1 + B)^n(1 + B^{-1})^n + \lambda(1 - B)^n(1 - B^{-1})^n} \tag{4.20}$$

Expressions (4.19) and (4.20) require a value for λ for them to become operational. Consider again the trend filter (4.19). By some fairly tortuous algebra, this can be written as

$$\psi_T(z) = \frac{1}{1 + \lambda\big(i(1-z)/(1+z)\big)^{2n}}$$

and setting $z = \exp(-i\omega)$ yields the frequency response function

$$\psi_T(e^{-i\omega}) = \frac{1}{1 + \lambda\big(i(1-e^{-i\omega})/(1+e^{-i\omega})\big)^{2n}} \tag{4.21}$$

Now,

$$i\frac{(1-e^{-i\omega})}{(1+e^{-i\omega})} = i\frac{(e^{i\omega/2} - e^{-i\omega/2})}{(e^{i\omega/2} + e^{-i\omega/2})}$$

Using the Euler equations (4.5), this becomes

$$i^2 \frac{\sin(\omega/2)}{\cos(\omega/2)} = -\tan(\omega/2)$$

Thus (4.21) can be written

$$\psi_T(e^{-i\omega}) = \frac{1}{1 + \lambda\big(\tan(\omega/2)\big)^{2n}} \tag{4.22}$$

If we wish the filter to pass all frequencies up to a cut-off of ω_c, then, because the filter is symmetric, we should set ω_c such that the gain is 0.5. Solving (4.22) for this value gives

$$\lambda = \big(1/\tan(\omega_c/2)\big)^{2n}$$

The 'smoothing parameter' λ is thus dependent on n and ω_c. Setting these parameters too low will make the fitted trend unreasonably smooth to offer a realistic decomposition of y_t, while setting them too high will make the trend overly responsive to short-term (high-frequency) fluctuations in the observed series. The choice of the

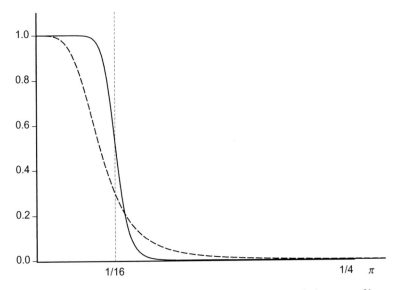

Figure 4.7 Frequency response functions for Butterworth low-pass filter with $n = 6$ and $\omega_c = \pi/16$ (——) and *H–P* trend filter with $\lambda = 1,600$ (– – –)

order n and the cut-off frequency ω_c may then be based on, for example, an examination of the spectral density of y_t, or on general considerations of goodness and smoothness of fit of the resulting trend estimate $\hat{\mu}_t$. Typical values of n are 4 and 6, while the range of the cut-off frequency is usually $0.05 \leq \omega_c \leq 0.40$, i.e., approximately $\pi/64$ to $\pi/8$.

Figure 4.7 shows the frequency response functions of the Butterworth low-pass (trend) filter for $\omega_c = \pi/16$ and $n = 6$, and the *H–P*(1600) trend filter, which corresponds to the same cut-off frequency. The Butterworth filter's frequency response shows a more rapid transition from unity to zero, so that it passes much less of the frequencies that it is designed to suppress than the *H–P* filter.

Further Reading and Background Material

4.1 The frequency-domain properties of linear filters are set out in various texts. Harvey (1993) is an accessible source, while Pollock (1999) is a compendium of detail. Osborn (1995) contains a useful exposition of detrending using moving averages, while Baxter and King (1999) and Pollock (2000) set out the theory of band-pass filtering, which was first proposed by Craddock (1957).

4.2 The *H–P* filter was first proposed in the economics literature by Hodrick and Prescott in a working paper in 1980, although they remark that it has a long history of use in, for example, actuarial science, where it is known as the Whittaker–Henderson Type A method of smoothing mortality (see Whittaker, 1923). The working paper was finally published, almost unaltered, some seventeen years later as Hodrick and Prescott (1997). The analysis of this section is based on several papers that investigate the implications and various aspects of the *H–P* filter, most notably King and Rebelo (1993), Harvey and Jaeger (1993), Cogley and Nason (1995) and Pedersen (2001). The *H–P* filter is now a common routine programmed into many econometric software packages.

4.3 The Butterworth filter has a long history of use in electrical engineering: see, for example, Pollock (1999). Its use for detrending economic time series has been proposed by Pollock (2000, 2001a, 2001b), where a procedure for tackling the finite sample problem is developed. This requires specialised programs to be used: see the above references for details.

5
Nonlinear and Nonparametric Trend Modelling

5.1 Regime shift models

5.1.1 Markov models

Consider once again the basic trend-cycle UC decomposition $y_t = \mu_t + \varepsilon_t$, but where the trend component now follows the process

$$\mu_t = \beta(m_t) + \mu_{t-1} = \beta_0 + \beta_1 m_t + \mu_{t-1} \tag{5.1}$$

μ_t is again a nonstationary random walk component, but its drift now evolves according to a two-state Markov process having transition probabilities

$$P(m_t = 0 \mid m_{t-1} = 0) = p$$
$$P(m_t = 1 \mid m_{t-1} = 0) = 1 - p$$
$$P(m_t = 0 \mid m_{t-1} = 1) = 1 - q$$
$$P(m_t = 1 \mid m_{t-1} = 1) = q$$

Thus $\Delta\mu_t$ need not change every period, as it does in conventional UC formulations, but responds only to occasional, discrete events. Note that if $p = 1 - q$, m_t is then a two-point random variable, taking the values 0 and 1, with probabilities $1 - q$ and q, independently of the previous values of the process, rather than a zero mean random variable drawn from a continuous distribution such as the normal. Let us now define the two random variables

$$\xi_{kt} = \begin{cases} 1 & \text{when } m_t = k \\ 0 & \text{when } m_t \neq k \end{cases} \qquad k = 0, 1$$

Then

$$E(\xi_{0t}) = p\xi_{0,t-1} + (1-q)\xi_{1,t-1}$$
$$E(\xi_{1t}) = (1-p)\xi_{0,t-1} + q\xi_{1,t-1}$$

or

$$\begin{bmatrix} \xi_{0t} \\ \xi_{1t} \end{bmatrix} = \begin{bmatrix} p & 1-q \\ 1-p & q \end{bmatrix} \begin{bmatrix} \xi_{0,t-1} \\ \xi_{1,t-1} \end{bmatrix} + \begin{bmatrix} \nu_{0t} \\ \nu_{1t} \end{bmatrix} \tag{5.2}$$

where $\nu_{it} = \xi_{it} - E(\xi_{it})$, $i = 0, 1$. Noting that $\xi_{1t} = m_t$ and $\xi_{0t} = 1 - \xi_{1t} = 1 - m_t$, (5.2) implies that m_t has the strictly stationary AR(1) representation

$$m_t = \lambda_0 + \lambda_1 m_{t-1} + \nu_t \tag{5.3}$$

where $\lambda_0 = 1 - p$, $\lambda_1 = p + q - 1$, and where the innovation ν_t has the conditional probability distribution

$$P(\nu_t = (1-p)|m_{t-1} = 0) = p$$
$$P(\nu_t = -p|m_{t-1} = 0) = 1 - p$$
$$P(\nu_t = -(1-q)|m_{t-1} = 1) = q$$
$$P(\nu_t = q|m_{t-1} = 1) = 1 - q$$

Thus the trend component has the ARIMA(1, 1, 0) representation

$$(1 - \lambda_1 B)\Delta\mu_t = \theta_0 + a_t$$

where $\theta = \beta_0 - \beta_0\lambda_1 + \beta_1\lambda_0$ and $a_t = \beta_1\nu_t$ is an innovation with a rather unusual probability distribution. While this innovation is uncorrelated with lagged values of m_t since

$$E\left(\nu_t | m_{t-j} = 0\right) = E\left(\nu_t | m_{t-j} = 1\right) = 0 \quad \text{for } j \geqslant 1$$

it is not independent of such lagged values, since, for example,

$$E\left(v_t^2 \mid m_{t-1} = 0\right) = p(1-p)$$

but

$$E\left(v_t^2 \mid m_{t-1} = 1\right) = q(1-q)$$

Since the unconditional probabilities of being in a particular state, or regime, are

$$P(m_t = 0) = \frac{1-q}{2-p-q}, \quad P(m_t = 1) = \frac{1-p}{2-p-q}$$

it is straightforward to show that the variance of $\Delta\mu_t = \beta_0 + \beta_1 m_t$ is

$$\beta_1^2 \frac{(1-p)(1-q)}{(2-p-q)^2}$$

This variance will be zero if either p or q is unity, in which case μ_t will then become the deterministic linear trend $\mu_t = \alpha_0 + \alpha_1 t$, where $\alpha_1 = \beta_0$ or $\beta_0 + \beta_1$ depending on whether q or p equals unity.

We may also ask the question: given that we are currently in regime j ($m_t = j$, $j = 0, 1$), how long, on average, will regime j last? If we define D as the duration of state 0, then

$$D = 1, \text{ if } m_t = 0 \text{ and } m_{t+1} = 1; \ P(D=1) = 1-p$$
$$D = 2, \text{ if } m_t = m_{t+1} = 0 \text{ and } m_{t+2} = 1; \ P(D=2) = p(1-p),$$
$$D = 3, \text{ if } m_t = m_{t+1} = m_{t+2} = 0 \text{ and } m_{t+3} = 1; \ P(D=3) = p^2(1-p)$$

so that the expected duration of regime 0 is given by

$$E(D) = \sum_{i=1}^{\infty} iP(D=i) = (1-p)\sum_{i=1}^{\infty} ip^{i-1} = (1-p)^{-1}$$

since

$$\sum_{i=1}^{\infty} ip^{i-1} = (1-p)^{-2}$$

using standard results on arithmetico-geometric progressions. By an identical argument, the expected duration of regime 1 is $(1-q)^{-1}$.

The cycle component ε_t may be assumed to follow an AR(r) process

$$\phi(B)\varepsilon_t = u_t$$

where u_t is white noise with variance σ^2 and, unlike the conventional UC specification, $\phi(B)$ can contain a unit root. Thus, if μ_t is a deterministic linear trend and $\phi(B)$ does contain a unit root, y_t will be a DS process, whereas if $\phi(B)$ does not contain a unit root, y_t will be TS.

Suppose that $\phi(B)$ does contain a unit root, so that it can be written $\phi(B) = \phi^*(B)\Delta$. The UC decomposition of y_t is then

$$\phi^*(B)\Delta(y_t - \mu_t) = \phi^*(B)(\Delta y_t - \mu_t^*) = u_t \tag{5.5}$$

where

$$\mu_t^* = \Delta\mu_t = \beta_0 + \beta_1 m_t$$

This can be written as

$$\mu_t^* = \mu_0^*(1 - m_t) + \mu_1^* m_t$$

where $\mu_0^* = \beta_0$ and $\mu_1^* = \beta_0 + \beta_1$ can be interpreted as the expected growth rates of y_t in the two regimes.

Although relatively simple, the Markov-regime switching model cannot be estimated by conventional techniques and requires special algorithms. Schematically, the model can be estimated by maximum likelihood on using (5.1) to write $\Delta\varepsilon_t = \Delta y_t - \Delta\mu_t$ as

$$\varepsilon_t = \varepsilon_{t-1} + y_t - y_{t-1} - \beta_0 - \beta_1 m_t$$

and solving backwards in time to yield

$$\varepsilon_t = y_t - y_0 - \beta_0 t - \beta_1 \sum_{i=1}^{t} m_i + \varepsilon_0 \tag{5.6}$$

Using (5.4) and (5.6), the innovations u_t can be expressed as

$$\begin{aligned} u_t &= \phi(B)(y_t - y_0 - \beta_0 t) + \phi(1)\varepsilon_0 - \beta_1\phi(1)\sum_{i=1}^{t} m_i \\ &\quad + \beta_1 \sum_{j=1}^{r}\left(\sum_{k=j}^{r}\phi_k\right)m_{t-j+1} \end{aligned}$$

Assuming that the u_t are normal, this expression can be utilised to calculate the log likelihood function on noting that this can be decomposed as the sum of the conditional (on past observations) log likelihoods. These conditional log likelihoods depend on unobserved current and past realisations of the Markov states m_t. A recursive relationship can be shown to hold between the conditional distribution of the states and the conditional likelihood of the observations and this can be exploited to obtain an algorithm for evaluating the log likelihood function. Inferences about the unobserved components and states are then obtained as byproducts of this evaluation.

Example 5.1: A Markov switching model for US output

The model given by (5.5) was fitted to the US output series analysed in previous examples with $\phi^*(B) = 1 - \phi^*B$, producing the estimates (standard errors in parentheses)

$$\hat{\mu}_0 = -1.022 \qquad \hat{\mu}_1 = 0.785 \qquad p = 0.638 \qquad q = 0.962$$
$$\phantom{\hat{\mu}_0 = }(0.274) \qquad \phantom{\hat{\mu}_1 = }(0.084)$$

$$\hat{\phi}^* = 0.272 \qquad \hat{\sigma}^2 = 0.528$$
$$\phantom{\hat{\phi}^* = }(0.062)$$

Thus state 0 has an expected growth rate of -1.02 per cent per quarter (approximately -4 per cent per annum) and so can be characterised as the contractionary regime, while state 1 (the expansionary regime) has an expected growth rate of 0.78 per cent per quarter (3 per cent per annum). The expected durations of the two regimes are $(1 - 0.638)^{-1} = 2.8$ quarters and $(1 - 0.962)^{-1} = 26.3$ quarters, respectively, so that contractions are extremely short (on average eight months) compared to the expected duration of an expansion of between 6 and 7 years. Deviations from average growth in the two regimes follow a positively autocorrelated AR(1) process.

5.1.2 STAR models

The Markov chain models assume that the regime that the series is in at time t depends upon an unobservable state variable. An alternative class of models allows the regime to be determined by an observable variable, q_t. If the regime is determined by the value q_t

relative to a *threshold value*, say c, then we have a *threshold autoregressive* (TAR) model. If the threshold variable is a lagged value of the series itself, so that $q_t = y_{t-k}$ for some integer $k > 0$, then the model is called a *self-exciting* TAR (SETAR).

For example, with a delay of $k = 1$ and an AR(1) model assumed for both of the two regimes, the SETAR model is given by

$$y_t = \begin{cases} \phi_{01} + \phi_{11}y_{t-1} + \varepsilon_t & \text{if } y_{t-1} \leqslant c \\ \phi_{02} + \phi_{12}y_{t-1} + \varepsilon_t & \text{if } y_{t-1} > c \end{cases} \tag{5.7}$$

An alternative way of writing (5.7) is

$$y_t = (\phi_{01} + \phi_{11}y_{t-1})(1 - I[y_{t-1} > c]) + (\phi_{02} + \phi_{12}y_{t-1})I[y_{t-1} > c] + \varepsilon_t \tag{5.8}$$

where $I[A] = 1$ if the event A occurs and $I[A] = 0$ otherwise.

The SETAR model assumes that the 'boundary' between the two regimes is given by the specific value c. A more gradual transition between the two regimes is allowed by generalising (5.8) by replacing $I[y_{t-1} > c]$ with a continuous function, say $S_t(y_{t-1})$, which changes smoothly and monotonically from 0 to 1 as y_{t-1} increases. Such a function has been introduced in Chapter 2 (see (2.14)) to model a smooth transition between two trend regimes and can easily be adapted here to define the smooth transition AR (STAR) model. The logistic function

$$S_t(y_{t-1}) = \left(1 + \exp(-\gamma(y_{t-1} - c))\right)^{-1} \tag{5.9}$$

allows (5.8) to be rewritten as the logistic STAR (LSTAR) model

$$y_t = (\phi_{01} + \phi_{11}y_{t-1})(1 - S_t(y_{t-1})) + (\phi_{02} + \phi_{12}y_{t-1})S_t(y_{t-1}) + \varepsilon_t$$

The parameter c now has the interpretation of being the midpoint of the transition, since $S_t(c) = 0.5$. The parameter γ controls the speed of the transition between regimes. For large values of γ, $S_t(y_{t-1})$ approaches the indicator function $I[y_{t-1} > c]$, so that the SETAR is nested within the LSTAR. Indeed, when $\gamma = 0$, $S_t(y_{t-1}) = 0.5$, so that a linear AR(1) model results. If y_t is a growth rate and c is close to zero, $S_t(y_{t-1}) = 1$ defines an expansionary regime and $S_t(y_{t-1}) = 0$ a contractionary regime, with both regimes able to have different dynamics.

Of course, c does not have to be near zero and, if it is positive, the two regimes may be characterised as 'normal' and 'low' growth, for example. Yet another way of writing the model is as

$$y_t = \left[\phi_{01} + \pi_0 S_t(y_{t-1})\right] + \left[\phi_{11} + \pi_1 S_t(y_{t-1})\right]y_{t-1} + \varepsilon_t \qquad (5.10)$$

where $\pi_i = \phi_{i2} - \phi_{i1}$, $i = 0$, 1. This form perhaps shows more clearly that estimation can be carried out be NLS.

While the logistic function is a popular choice of smooth transition, an alternative is available in the form of the exponential function

$$V(y_{t-1}) = 1 - \exp\left(-\gamma(y_{t-1} - c)^2\right) \qquad (5.11)$$

Use of this function defines the exponential STAR (ESTAR) model. Examples of the two functions are shown in Figure 5.1. This reveals that, for the ESTAR model, only the distance from the location parameter is important, so that regimes are effectively defined by values close to c and far from c. In some circumstances, however, the ESTAR model can have similar implications to the LSTAR specification. This is when almost all of the observations lie to the right of the location parameter, in which case the effective distinction between the two models is the shape of the transition function.

The logistic function is symmetric around $y_{t-1} = c$. Suppose that at $y_{t-1}^a = c + z$, $S_t(y_{t-1}^a) = \lambda > 0.5$. At $y_{t-1}^b = c - z$, this symmetry implies that $S_t(y_{t-1}^b) = 1 - \lambda$, with the derivatives $\partial S_t(y_{t-1})/\partial y_{t-1}$ equal at these two points, which leads to a corresponding symmetry in the coefficients $\phi_{i1} + \pi_i S_t(y_{t-1})$, $i = 0$, 1, of the LSTAR model (5.10). An implication of this is that these coefficients change, as functions of y_{t-1}, at the same rate irrespective of whether the series is in the recessionary state (with $S_t(y_{t-1})$ close to zero) or whether it is in an expansionary state with $S_t(y_{t-1})$ close to unity. The right-hand half of the exponential function (5.11), on the other hand, does not have this property. Differentiating (5.11) yields

$$Z(y_{t-1}) = \frac{\partial V_t(y_{t-1})}{\partial y_{t-1}} = 2\gamma(y_{t-1} - c)\exp\left(-\gamma(y_{t-1} - c)^2\right)$$

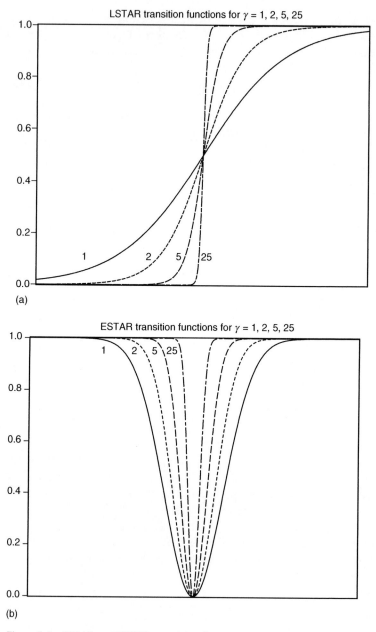

Figure 5.1 LSTAR and ESTAR transition functions

If $V_t(y_{t-1}^a) = \lambda > 0.5$, then this derivative can be written as $2(1 - \lambda)\sqrt{-\gamma \ln(1 - \lambda)}$. It can then be verified that the derivative at $1 - \lambda$ will always be greater than that at λ. Consequently, the rate of change in the coefficients $\phi_{i1} + \pi_i S_t(y_{t-1})$ will be sharper when y_{t-1} moves away from c (i.e., a transition from contraction to expansion) than when y_{t-1} moves towards c from a distance. This property of ESTAR models may be useful in capturing the asymmetries that have been well documented to occur in business cycles.

Two extensions to STAR models are to allow for underlying $AR(p)$ models and, of course, to allow for an arbitrary delay parameter k. Additional transition functions can also be included, but we will consider the specification problem posed by having to determine the AR lag length p, the form of the transition function (either logistic or exponential), and the delay k. The specification procedure can be split into three steps:

(i) Specify the appropriate linear $AR(p)$ model to form the starting point for further analysis.
(ii) Test linearity against STAR using the linear model in (i) as the null model; if linearity is rejected, the delay parameter k can then be determined
(iii) Conditional upon k, choose between an LSTAR and an ESTAR specification.

Assuming that an $AR(p)$ model has been selected by usual procedures as the first step, the null of linearity can be tested in the following way. Consider the regression

$$y_t = \sum_{i=1}^{p} \varphi_i y_{t-i} + \sum_{j=1}^{p} \delta_{1j} y_{t-j} y_{t-k} + \sum_{j=1}^{p} \delta_{2j} y_{t-j} y_{t-k}^2$$
$$+ \sum_{j=1}^{p} \delta_{3j} y_{t-j} y_{t-k}^3 + \nu_t \tag{5.12}$$

This may be regarded as a third-order Taylor approximation to an LSTAR model with p lags. The linearity hypothesis when the alternative is LSTAR is thus $H_0 : \delta_{ij} = 0$, for all i and j. This test is, of course, conditional on the delay parameter k being known. When unknown, it may be chosen on the basis of a sequence of tests of H_0 for alternative values of k: we choose the value that minimises the probability value of the individual tests in the sequence.

Assuming that H_0 is rejected, we may then choose between an LSTAR and an ESTAR specification by the following procedure. First test whether all 'fourth-order' terms are insignificant, i.e., test $H_0^{(4)}$: $\delta_{3j} = 0$ for all j. Next, conditional on $H_0^{(4)}$, test the significance of all 'third-order' terms, $H_0^{(3)}$: $\delta_{2j} = 0 | \delta_{3j} = 0$. Finally, conditional on $H_0^{(3)}$, test the significance of the 'second-order' terms, $H_0^{(2)}$: $\delta_{1j} = 0 | \delta_{2j} = \delta_{3j} = 0$. If the test of $H_0^{(3)}$ has the smallest probability value of the three tests, choose the ESTAR specification, if not, choose the LSTAR model.

Example 5.2: A STAR model for UK output

The above specification procedure was followed for the (logarithms of the) quarterly postwar UK output series analysed in previous examples. Although the series is characterised by a drifting random walk, we deliberately began with an overfitted AR(1) linear model for the differences Δy_t. Estimating (5.12) with $p = 1$ and $k = 1, \ldots, 4$ yielded probability values for testing H_0 of 0.038, 0.989, 0.937 and 0.020, respectively, thus selecting a delay of $k = 4$. Conditional on this setting, probability values of 0.092, 0.014 and 0.331 were then obtained for the hypotheses $H_0^{(i)}$, $i = 4, 3, 2$, thus selecting an ESTAR specification as $H_0^{(3)}$ has the smallest probability value.

The subsequently fitted ESTAR model is

$$\Delta y_t = -0.0057 + 0.0122 V_t(\Delta y_{t-4})$$
$$\quad\quad (0.0051)\ (0.0052)$$

$$+ \left(\begin{array}{c} -0.535 + 0.518 V_t(\Delta y_{t-4}) \\ (0.430)\ (0.442) \end{array} \right) \Delta y_{t-1} + \varepsilon_t$$

where

$$V_t(\Delta y_{t-4}) = 1 - \exp\left(-158503 \left(\Delta y_{t-4} + 0.0113 \atop (0.0012) \right)^2 \right)$$

A standard error is not provided for $\hat{\gamma}$ as the point estimate of this parameter is usually rather imprecise: an estimate of this size implies a rapid transition between the two regimes. Note that several of the other parameters are insignificant, particularly those related to Δy_{t-1}, which reflects the initial overfitting. A more parsimonious specification is

$$\Delta y_t = 0.0063 \, V_t(\Delta y_{t-4}) + \varepsilon_t$$
$$(0.0008)$$

$$V_t(\Delta y_{t-4}) = 1 - \exp\left(-104856\left(\Delta y_{t-4} + \underset{(0.0025)}{0.0114}\right)^2\right)$$

This specification can be written as

$$\Delta y_t = \begin{cases} \varepsilon_t & \text{if } \Delta y_{t-4} \leq -0.0114 \\ 0.0063 + \varepsilon_t & \text{if } \Delta y_{t-4} > -0.0114 \end{cases}$$

Thus the threshold is a decline in output of 1.14 per cent (approximately 4.6 per cent per annum) four quarters previously. The 'contractionary' regime is thus a driftless random walk, while the 'normal' regime is that of a random walk with a drift of 0.63 per cent (approximately 2.5 per cent per annum), which is close to what is usually thought to be the long-run trend growth rate of the UK economy.

Interestingly, the analogous LSTAR model is estimated as

$$\Delta y_t = 0.0064 \, S_t(\Delta y_{t-4}) + \varepsilon_t$$
$$(0.0008)$$

$$S_t(\Delta y_{t-4}) = \left(1 + \exp\left(-2798\left(\Delta y_{t-4} + \underset{(0.0026)}{0.0069}\right)\right)\right)^{-1}$$

The fits of the two models are very similar, with the residual standard errors being 0.0104 for the ESTAR and 0.0105 for the LSTAR models, respectively, and the two regimes are virtually identical in both models. The central parts of the estimated transition functions are shown in Figure 5.2 and the difference between the two transitions is clearly seen. The LSTAR model shows a rapid transition between the two regimes with a midpoint at $c = -0.007$. The ESTAR model has $c = -0.011$ and, as discussed above, the right-hand side of the transition is steeper below 0.5 than it is above it, thus indicating that UK output growth displays business cycle asymmetry.

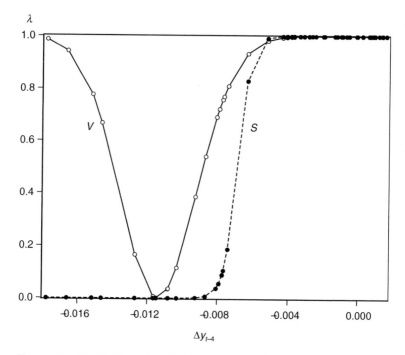

Figure 5.2   LSTAR (*S*) and ESTAR (*V*) transition functions for UK output growth

5.2   Nonparametric trends

5.2.1   Smoothing estimators

Consider the situation where we wish to fit a very general trend function to a time series y_t, i.e.

$$y_t = f(t) + \varepsilon_t \tag{5.13}$$

where $f(t)$ is not constrained to belong to a specific class of trend functions, e.g., linear, polynomial or a smooth transition.

How might the unknown function $f(\cdot)$ be estimated? Consider a particular date $t = \tau$ and suppose that, for this one observation, we can obtain *repeated* independent observations of y_τ, say $y_\tau^1, y_\tau^2, ..., y_\tau^n$:

i.e., there are n independent realisations of y at the same date τ. A natural estimator of the function $f(t)$ at τ is then

$$\hat{f}(\tau) = \frac{1}{n}\sum_{i=1}^{n} y_\tau^i = \frac{1}{n}\sum_{i=1}^{n}\left(f(\tau) + \varepsilon_\tau^i\right) = f(\tau) + \frac{1}{n}\sum_{i=1}^{n}\varepsilon_\tau^i \qquad (5.14)$$

where we have defined $\varepsilon_\tau^i = y_\tau^i - f(\tau)$. By the Law of Large Numbers the final term $n^{-1}\Sigma\varepsilon_\tau$ becomes negligible for large n.

Clearly this approach is an impossibility in practice but, if we assume that the function $f(t)$ is sufficiently 'smooth', then for dates near to τ, the corresponding values of y_t should be close to $f(\tau)$. Thus in a small neighbourhood around τ, $f(\tau)$ will be nearly constant and may be estimated by taking an average of the y_ts that correspond to those dates that are near τ. The closer the dates are to τ, the closer an average of the corresponding y_ts will be to $f(\tau)$, which suggests that a *weighted* average of the y_ts, where the weights decline as the dates get farther away from τ, should be used. This weighted-average, or 'local averaging', procedure of estimating $f(t)$ is the essence of nonparametric regression, or *smoothing* as it is often called in the present context.

More formally, a smoothing estimator of $f(\tau)$ is defined as

$$\hat{f}(\tau) = \frac{1}{T}\sum_{t=1}^{T}\omega_t(\tau)y_t \qquad (5.15)$$

where the weights $\omega_t(\tau)$ are large for those y_ts with dates near τ, and small for those y_ts with dates far from τ. To implement such a procedure, 'near' and 'far' need to be defined. If we choose too large a neighbourhood around τ with which to compute the average, the estimate $\hat{f}(\tau)$ will be too smooth and will not exhibit any genuine nonlinearities existing in $f(\tau)$. On the other hand, too small a neighbourhood will make $\hat{f}(\tau)$ too variable, reflecting noise as well as the variations in $f(\tau)$. The weights $\omega_t(\tau)$ must therefore be carefully chosen to balance these two considerations.

5.2.2 Kernel regression

The *kernel regression* estimator uses a weight function constructed from a probability density function $K(u)$, or *kernel*, such that

$$K(u) \geq 0, \quad \int K(u)du = 1 \quad \int uK(u)du = 0 \quad \int u^2K(u)du > 0$$

By rescaling the kernel with respect to a parameter $h > 0$, we can change its spread, i.e., if we define

$$K_h(u) \equiv h^{-1}K(u/h), \quad \int K_h(u)du = 1$$

we can then define the weight function to be used in (5.15) as

$$\omega_{t,h}(\tau) = \frac{K_h(\tau - t)}{T^{-1}\sum_{t=1}^{T}K_h(\tau - t)} \tag{5.16}$$

If h is small (large), averaging will be done with respect to a small (large) neighbourhood around τ. Controlling the degree of averaging thus amounts to adjusting h, which is therefore known as the smoothing parameter, or the *bandwidth*. Substituting (5.16) into (5.15) yields the *Nadaraya–Watson* kernel estimator

$$\hat{f}_h(\tau) = \frac{1}{T}\sum_{t=1}^{T}\omega_{t,h}(\tau)y_t = \frac{\sum_{t=1}^{T}K_h(\tau - t)y_t}{\sum_{t=1}^{T}K_h(\tau - t)} \tag{5.17}$$

Under a wide range of conditions on the shape of the kernel and the behaviour of the weights as the sample size T grows, $\hat{f}_h(\tau)$ converges to $f(\tau)$. A popular choice of kernel is the Gaussian

$$K_h(\tau) = \frac{1}{h\sqrt{2\pi}}\exp(-\tau^2/2h^2)$$

although various other kernels are available.

The estimator (5.17) is a function of the single parameter h, the bandwidth. Various methods are available for selecting the most appropriate value of this parameter, but they are typically variants of minimising the within-sample fit subject to restrictions on the degree of variability/smoothness of the fitted function. These can be rather difficult to use in empirical applications and perhaps the best approach is to try a range of values and select the one that provides the most satisfactory trend for the series at hand, or to use a general default value for h. A widely used default uses the formula

$h_d = 0.75s/T^{0.2}$, where s^2 is the variance of the 'regressor' variable. When the regressor is a time trend, this variance can be shown to be $s^2 = (T - 1)(T + 1)/12 \approx T^2/12$, so that $h_d = (\sqrt{3}/8)T^{0.8}$. Thus, for example, when $T = 100$, $h_d = 8.6$, while for $T = 500$, $h_d = 31.3$.

5.2.3   Local polynomial regression

The form of (5.17) shows that $\hat{f}_h(\tau)$ can be considered as the solution to a weighted least squares problem, being the minimiser $\hat{\beta}_0$ of

$$Q_0 = \Sigma_{t=1}^T (y_t - \beta_0)^2 K_h(\tau - t)$$

In other words, $\hat{f}_h(\tau)$ corresponds to locally approximating $f(\tau)$ with a constant. The Nadaraya–Watson kernel estimator is most natural for a random sample of data, which may not be appropriate in the current application, where the time trend t is a 'fixed design'. Moreover, a local constant usually makes sense only over a very small neighbourhood. These considerations suggest fitting higher-order local polynomials as approximations to $f(\tau)$: a pth-order *local polynomial regression estimator* is the minimiser of

$$Q_p = \Sigma_{t=1}^T \left(y_t - \beta_0 - \beta_1(\tau - t) - ...\beta_p(\tau - t)^p\right)^2 K_h(\tau - t)$$

Apart from choosing the kernel and the bandwidth h, the choice of polynomial order p needs to be determined. It has been shown that odd-order polynomials have clear advantages over even-order ones, particularly in the boundary regions (i.e., at the start and end of the sample period).

Example 5.3: Nonparametric trends in US stock prices

Figure 5.3 superimposes local cubic ($p = 3$) trends using a Gaussian kernel on the S&P 500 stock market index. Panel (a) uses a bandwidth of $h = 2$, which produces a trend almost identical to the Henderson MA trend shown in Figure 2.6. With $T = 131$ here, panel (b) uses $h_d = 10.7$ and a much smoother trend results. Figure 5.4 shows the annual trend growth rates for the two bandwidths: obviously the higher setting of h produces much more stable trend growth.

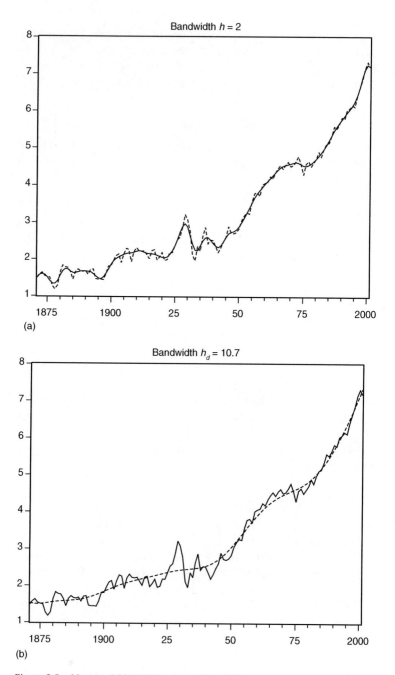

Figure 5.3 Nominal S&P 500 index (1871–2001), with local cubic trends

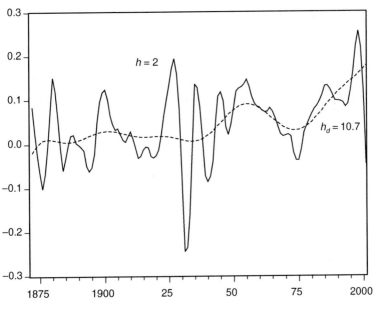

Figure 5.4   S&P 500 trend growth rates

5.3   Nonlinear stochastic trends

Consider again the random walk with drift model

$$y_t = y_{t-1} + g + a_t = gt + \sum_{j=0}^{t} a_{t-j} \qquad (5.18)$$

where $g > 0$ and a_t is white noise but with a possibly heteroscedastic variance $E(a_t^2) = \sigma_t^2$. This series will have mean $E(y_t) = gt$ and variance $\sigma^2(y) = \sum_{j=0}^{t} \sigma_t^2$. A more general model is

$$y_t = y_{t-1} + g(y_{t-1}) + a_t \qquad (5.19)$$

where

$$g(y) = cy^\alpha, \qquad \alpha < 1$$

and

$$\sigma^2(y) = vy^\beta, \qquad \beta < \alpha + 1$$

so that the model can be written

$$\Delta y_t = cy_{t-1}^{\alpha} + \sqrt{vy_{t-1}^{\beta}} \cdot u_t \tag{5.20}$$

where u_t has zero mean and unit variance. The conditions on the parameters ensure that the model is a 'growth process', i.e., that y_t tends to infinity as t increases with unit probability.

Estimation of (5.20) can be carried out using maximum likelihood techniques, and a nonparametric approach is available if we write (5.19) as

$$\Delta y_t = g(y_{t-1}) + a_t$$

and use the techniques discussed in section 5.2.

Further Reading and Background Material

5.1 Markov processes were first introduced to model regime shifts and the business cycle by Hamilton (1989) and extended by Lam (1990). Details of estimation algorithms may also be found in Hamilton (1990, 1994) and Kim and Nelson (1999), where detailed analysis of Markov models and their many extensions is also provided.

SETAR and STAR models were introduced in Tong and Lim (1980) and Chan and Tong (1986), while the methodology of building STAR models was developed by Teräsvirta and Anderson (1992) and Teräsvirta (1994). A convenient textbook reference for these models is Granger and Teräsvirta (1993), while Teräsvirta (1998) is a recent and comprehensive review.

5.2 Nonparametric regression is a major research area of econometrics: see, for example, the text by Härdle (1990) and the more recent review of Yatchew (1998). Nonparametric trend modelling, however, is still rather uncommon, although Lo, Mamaysky and Wang (2000) provide an interesting financial application of kernel regression. Simonoff (1996) is a good general introduction to the area, which also includes such related techniques as nearest neighbour and projection pursuit. The package *Econometric Views* contains useful routines for computing nonparametric trends using these procedures.

5.3 Stochastic nonlinear models were introduced into the econometrics literature by Granger, Inoue and Morin (1997), where detailed technical analysis may be found. A related model is the bounded random walk analysed by Nicolau (2002). So far little use has been made of them, and we can offer no examples, but this may change in the future.

6

Multivariate Modelling of Trends and Cycles

6.1 Common features in time series

6.1.1 Specification and testing of common features

It is often the case that we wish to model the trend and cyclical features of a group of time series. For example, as was pointed out in Chapter 1, an implication of neoclassical growth theory is that consumption, investment and output share a common stochastic trend component produced by a single technology shock to the production function. Such a model can also be used to show that common cyclical components may also result. How might such common components be formalised? A general framework may be developed by considering two time series, y_{1t} and y_{2t}, generated by the following model

$$
\begin{aligned}
y_{1t} &= \lambda \omega_t + \varepsilon_{1t} \\
y_{2t} &= \omega_t + \varepsilon_{2t}
\end{aligned}
\tag{6.1}
$$

Here ω_t is a variable common to both y_{1t} and y_{2t} that has a particular statistical property that the components ε_{1t} and ε_{2t} do not share. Such a property, or *feature*, could be a trend, a seasonal pattern, serial correlation, etc. More formally, we can propose three properties that such a feature should have: (i) if y_{1t} has (does not have) the feature, then λy_{1t} will have (will not have) the feature for any $\lambda \neq 0$; (ii) if y_{1t} and y_{2t} do not have the feature, then $z_t = y_{1t} + y_{2t}$ will not have the feature; and (iii) if y_{1t} does not have the feature but y_{2t} does have it, then $z_t = y_{1t} + y_{2t}$ will also have the feature.

These three properties do not exhaust all possibilities, however, for they leave open the case when y_{1t} and y_{2t} both have the feature but z_t does not. If this is the case then the feature is said to be *common*. More generally, a feature that is present in each of a group of series, say $y_{1t}, y_{2t}, ..., y_{nt}$, is said to be common to those series if there exists a nonzero linear combination of the series, $z_t = \Sigma_{i=1}^n \delta_i y_{it}$, that does not have the feature. As a simple example, consider the linear trend feature, $\omega_t = \beta t$ in (6.1). Then

$$z_t = y_{1t} + \delta y_{2t} = (\lambda + \delta)\beta t + \varepsilon_{1t} + \delta \varepsilon_{2t}$$

which will be trend-free if $\delta = -\lambda$.

How can common features be tested for? A convenient regression approach is to generalise (6.1) to

$$\begin{aligned} y_{1t} &= x_t \beta_1 + w_t \lambda_1 + \varepsilon_{1t} \\ y_{2t} &= x_t \beta_2 + w_t \lambda_2 + \varepsilon_{2t} \end{aligned} \tag{6.2}$$

where x_t and w_t are k_x and k_w dimensional vectors of variables that influence both y_{1t} and y_{2t}, the latter containing the variables defining the potential common feature. For there to be such a common feature, we require that there exists a δ such that $\lambda = 0$ in the model

$$y_{1t} = \delta y_{2t} + x_t \beta + w_t \lambda + \varepsilon_t \tag{6.3}$$

A convenient way of ascertaining whether this is the case is to estimate (6.3) under the null $\lambda = 0$ by two-stage least squares (2SLS) to account for the 'endogeneity' induced by including y_{2t} as a regressor. This will produce the residuals $e_t = y_{1t} - \hat{\delta} y_{2t} - x_t \hat{\beta}$, $t = 1, 2, ..., T$, where $\hat{\delta}$ and $\hat{\beta}$ are the 2SLS estimates. The e_t are then regressed on x_t and w_t and $T \cdot R^2$ from this regression is computed. This is distributed as χ^2 with $k_w - 1$ degrees of freedom on the null $\lambda = 0$, so that large values of the test statistic, essentially a Lagrange Multiplier (LM) test, will lead to a rejection of the null of a common feature. Note that this approach will fail for simple common features. For example, if w_t contains just t then there are no degrees of freedom, reflecting the fact that, as was discussed above, a linear combination of the two series can always remove a linear trend.

More generally, if (6.2) contains n equations, then it can be written as

$$\mathbf{y}_t = \beta \mathbf{x}'_t + \lambda \mathbf{w}'_t + \varepsilon_t \tag{6.4}$$

where $\mathbf{y}_t = (y_{1t}, \ldots, y_{nt})'$ and λ is an $n \times k_w$ matrix that defines the feature to be found in the individual series: if the ith row of λ is 0, y_i does not show the feature. If there is a vector δ such that $\delta'\mathbf{y}_t$ does not have the feature, δ is called a *cofeature vector*. Any vector with the property $\delta'\lambda = 0$ will therefore be a cofeature vector. If there are r linearly independent cofeature vectors then the rank of λ must be $n - r$, although this is a restriction only if $k_w \geq n$. If the rank of λ is $n - r$, then it can be written as the product of two matrices also of rank $n - r$: $\lambda = \Lambda\Phi$, where Λ is $n \times (n - r)$ and Φ is $(n - r) \times k_w$. By defining $\mathbf{z}_t = \Phi\mathbf{w}'_t$, (6.4) can be rewritten as

$$\mathbf{y}_t - \beta \mathbf{x}'_t = \Lambda \mathbf{z}_t + \varepsilon_t \tag{6.5}$$

Since $\mathbf{z}_t$ is of dimension $n - r$, the n-dimensional $\mathbf{y}_t$ is thus a function of $n - r$ common components that exhibit the feature.

To test for a common feature in this multivariate setting, a natural generalisation of the LM testing approach is to extend (6.3) by the inclusion of $y_{3t}, \ldots, y_{nt}$, with the degrees of freedom of the test statistic being adjusted to $k_w - (n - 1)$. However, the implicit null and alternative hypotheses being tested here are $n - 1$ common features against n. If the null is that there are fewer than $n - 1$ common features, then the test statistic will not have the correct asymptotic size.

6.1.2 Common cycles and codependence

Working within the context of the model (6.3), the presence of a common cycle cofeature can be investigated by defining $\mathbf{w}_t$ to contain lags of y_{1t} and y_{2t}, with $\mathbf{x}_t$ containing, for example, a constant and possibly a time trend. The common cycle feature then has the interpretation that, although both series are serially correlated, there is a linear combination of them that is white noise, so that the serial correlation 'cancels out'. A more general concept is that of *codependence*. Suppose that $\mathbf{y}_t$ has a (stationary) vector MA (VMA) representation of order q, i.e., in (6.4) we assume that ε_t is (multivariate) white noise and $\mathbf{w}_t = (\varepsilon_{t-1}, \ldots, \varepsilon_{t-q})$, taking $\beta = 0$ for simplicity:

$$\mathbf{y}_t = \varepsilon_t + \lambda_1 \varepsilon_{t-1} + \ldots + \lambda_q \varepsilon_{t-q} \tag{6.6}$$

Since ε_t is $n \times 1$, the λ_i, $i = 1, \ldots, q$, are $n \times n$ coefficient matrices, with $k_w = nq$. The order of persistence of the process is q, since a shock to y lasts for only q periods before disappearing. In general, the order of persistence of the linear combination $\delta' \mathbf{y}_t$, defined as

$$\delta' \mathbf{y}_t = \delta' \varepsilon_t + \delta' \lambda_1 \varepsilon_{t-1} + \ldots + \delta' \lambda_q \varepsilon_{t-q}$$

will also be at most q. The time series making up $\mathbf{y}_t$ are then said to be codependent if this order of persistence is $q^* < q$, where $q^* + 1$ is the order of codependence. Codependence holds for (6.6) if $\delta' \lambda_{q^*} \neq 0$ but $\delta' \lambda_{q^*+j} = 0$ for $j > 0$.

An equivalent condition is in terms of the autocovariance matrices, $\Gamma(i) = E(\mathbf{y}_t \mathbf{y}_{t-i}')$. Codependence of order $q^* + 1$ requires that

$$\delta' \Gamma(q^* + 1) = \delta' \Gamma(q^* + 2) = \ldots = \delta' \Gamma(q) = 0$$

Related ideas hold for vector AR (VAR) processes. Suppose that $\mathbf{y}_t$ is generated by the VAR(2) process

$$\mathbf{y}_t = \phi_1 \mathbf{y}_{t-1} + \phi_2 \mathbf{y}_{t-2} + \varepsilon_t \tag{6.7}$$

This, of course, has an equivalent VMA(∞) representation. A common cycle feature exists if there is vector δ such that $\delta' \mathbf{y}_t = \varepsilon_t$, which requires that $\delta' \phi_1 = \delta' \phi_2 = 0$, but codependence is hardly of relevance unless q^* is very small. With this in mind, substitute for $\mathbf{y}_{t-1}$ in (6.7) to obtain

$$\mathbf{y}_t = (\phi_1^2 + \phi_2) \mathbf{y}_{t-2} + \phi_1 \phi_2 \mathbf{y}_{t-3} + \varepsilon_t + \phi_1 \varepsilon_{t-1}$$

Codependence of order $q^* = 1$ thus implies $\delta'(\phi_1^2 + \phi_2) = \delta' \phi_1 \phi_2 = 0$, so that

$$\delta' \mathbf{y}_t = \delta' \varepsilon_t + \delta' \phi_1 \varepsilon_{t-1}$$

This is alternatively referred to as a *nonsynchronous* common cycle.

Example 6.1: Is there a common cycle in US and Canadian output?

In this example we investigate whether there is a common cycle in quarterly US and Canadian output. We have already found in Example 3.3 that the logarithms of US output are well fitted by the ARIMA(1, 1, 0) process. Defining y_{1t} to be the first difference of the logarithms (i.e., output growth), fitting this model to the sample 1957.4 to 1999.4 obtained

$$y_{1t} = 0.0058 + 0.311 y_{1,t-1} + a_{1t}$$

Defining y_{2t} analogously for Canadian output growth, the following model was found to be appropriate for the same sample period

$$y_{2t} = 0.0047 + 0.255 y_{2,t-1} + 0.214 y_{2,t-2} + a_{2t}$$

Both series therefore exhibit a serial correlation 'feature' and thus are candidates to share a common cycle. With $\mathbf{w}_t$ defined to contain the first and second lags of y_{1t} and y_{2t} and $\mathbf{x}_t = 1$, 2SLS yielded the residuals $e_t = y_{1t} - 0.637 y_{2t} - 0.0028$ and regressing e_t on $\mathbf{x}_t$ and $\mathbf{w}_t$ produced a $T \cdot R^2$ statistic of 3.87. Since this is distributed as $\chi^2(2)$, we cannot reject the hypothesis that US and Canadian output growth share a common cycle. Indeed, examination of the SACF of e_t shows that it is indistinguishable from white noise.

6.1.3   Common deterministic trends

An important example of a common feature is a common deterministic trend. Consider the model (6.2) where $\omega_t = t$ and $\mathbf{x}_t = 1$:

$$\begin{aligned} y_{1t} &= \beta_1 + \lambda_1 t + \varepsilon_{1t} \\ y_{2t} &= \beta_2 + \lambda_2 t + \varepsilon_{2t} \end{aligned} \tag{6.8}$$

As discussed earlier, the LM approach fails in this case. A feasible way of testing for a common trend would be to estimate (6.8) as a system and to construct a Wald test, say, of the hypothesis $\lambda_1 = \lambda_2$. Serial and contemporaneous cross correlation in ε_{1t} and ε_{2t} can be

accounted for by autoregressive error corrections and system estimation techniques, respectively, while more complicated trend functions, for example, smooth transitions, can also be accommodated.

Example 6.2: Common trends in the Victorian economy

In Example 2.2 we found that the logarithm of UK output during
the Victorian period up to 1913 could be characterised as a trend
stationary process. This is also true of the logarithms of consumption and investment, as can be confirmed by carrying out the appropriate unit root tests. We now investigate whether the three series,
denoted y_t, c_t and i_t, respectively, share a common trend.

The following three-equation system was estimated for the period
1851–1913 by seemingly unrelated LS to take into account nonzero
contemporaneous error covariances:

$$y_t = \beta_1 + \lambda_1 t + \varepsilon_{1t}$$
$$c_t = \beta_2 + \lambda_2 t + \varepsilon_{2t}$$
$$i_t = \beta_3 + \lambda_3 t + \varepsilon_{3t}$$

with $\varepsilon_{it} = \phi_{i1}\varepsilon_{i,t-1} + \phi_{i2}\varepsilon_{i,t-2} + a_{it}$, $i = 1, 2, 3$. The trend parameters were
estimated as $\hat{\lambda}_1 = 0.0190$, $\hat{\lambda}_1 = 0.0181$ and $\hat{\lambda}_2 = 0.0214$, with standard
errors of 0.0005, 0.0009 and 0.0023, respectively. A Wald test of the
common trends hypothesis $\lambda_1 = \lambda_2 = \lambda_3$ produced a statistic of 2.92,
distributed as $\chi^2(2)$, which thus cannot reject the common trends
hypothesis. Estimating the system under this null produces a
common trends estimate of 0.0189 with a standard error of 0.0005.
Thus output, consumption and investment all grew at a trend rate
of 1.9 per cent per annum in the Victorian era. The series are shown
on a common scale in Figure 6.1, and the common trend is clearly
observed.

6.2 Common trends and cycles in a VAR framework

Suppose now that $\mathbf{y}_t$ can be represented by a VAR(p) process

$$\mathbf{y}_t = \mu + \Sigma_{i=1}^p \phi_i \mathbf{y}_{t-i} + \varepsilon_t = \mu + \phi(B)\mathbf{y}_{t-1} + \varepsilon_t \qquad (6.9)$$

where $\phi(B) = \Sigma_{i=1}^p \phi_i B^{i-1}$ is a matrix polynomial of lag coefficients. We
assume that the determinental equation $|\mathbf{I}_n - \phi(B)B| = 0$ has roots on

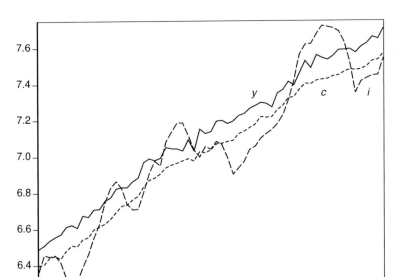

Figure 6.1 Output, consumption and income for the period 1851–1913

or outside the unit circle, i.e., $|B| \geq 1$, which precludes explosive processes but allows (6.9) to have some unit roots. We can write (6.9) as the (unrestricted) vector error correction model (VECM)

$$\Delta \mathbf{y}_t = \mu + \Pi \mathbf{y}_{t-1} + \sum_{i=1}^{p-1} \Gamma_i \Delta \mathbf{y}_{t-1} + \varepsilon_t = \mu + \Pi \mathbf{y}_{t-1} + \Gamma(B)\Delta \mathbf{y}_{t-1} + \varepsilon_t \tag{6.10}$$

where

$$\Gamma_i = -\sum_{j=i+1}^{p} \phi_j, \quad \Pi = \sum_{i=1}^{p} \phi_j - \mathbf{I}_n = \phi(1) - \mathbf{I}_n$$

The VECM (6.10) is merely an algebraic reexpression of the VAR (6.9). Two special cases, however, are of great importance. The first is when $\phi(1) = \mathbf{I}_n$ so that $\Pi = 0$ and $\Delta \mathbf{y}_t$ follows a VAR($p-1$) process. The condition $\phi(1) = \mathbf{I}_n$ also implies that $|\Pi| = 0$, in which case the VAR is said to contain *at least one* unit root. The converse does not necessarily hold, however, and this leads to the second special case.

$|\Pi| = 0$ implies that Π is of less than full rank, say $n - r$. Then, analogous to the earlier discussion, we can write Π as $\beta\alpha'$, where β and α are $n \times (n - r)$ matrices of full column rank. In this case y_t is said to have $n - r$ cointegrating vectors (the columns of α) and r unit roots. The $n - r$ dimensional vector $e_t = \alpha'y_t$ can be interpreted as an error correction, measuring the extent to which the system is out of equilibrium, and (6.10) can then be written as

$$\Delta \mathbf{y}_t = \mu + \beta \mathbf{e}_{t-1} + \sum_{i=1}^{p-1} \Gamma_i \Delta \mathbf{y}_{t-1} + \varepsilon_t = \mu + \beta \mathbf{e}_{t-1} + \Gamma(B)\Delta \mathbf{y}_{t-1} + \varepsilon_t \quad (6.11)$$

If it is assumed that $\Delta \mathbf{y}_t$ is stationary, then $\mathbf{e}_t = \alpha'\mathbf{y}_t$ must also be stationary for both sides of (6.11) to 'balance'. In other words, α' is a matrix whose rows, when post-multiplied by $\mathbf{y}_t$, produce stationary linear combinations of $\mathbf{y}_t$, i.e., the $n - r$ linear combinations $e_{it} = \alpha_i\mathbf{y}_t$, $i = 1, 2, ..., n - r$, are all stationary, where e_{it} and α_i are the ith rows of $\mathbf{e}_t$ and α'.

Since (6.9) can be written as

$$\left(\mathbf{I}_n - \phi(B)\right)\mathbf{y}_t = \mu + \varepsilon_t$$

$\Delta \mathbf{y}_t$ has the VMA(∞) representation

$$\Delta \mathbf{y}_t = C(B)(\mu + \varepsilon_t) \quad (6.12)$$

where

$$C(B) = \Delta\left(\mathbf{I}_n - \phi(B)\right)^{-1}$$

A useful way of expressing $C(B)$ is as

$$\begin{aligned}
C(B) &= \mathbf{I}_n + C_1 B + C_2 B^2 + ... \\
&= \mathbf{I}_n + C_1 + C_2 + ... + (C_1 B - C_1) + (C_2 B^2 - C_2) + ... \\
&= \mathbf{I}_n + C_1 + C_2 + ... \\
&\quad - \Delta\left(C_1 + C_2 + ... + (C_2 + C_3 + ...)B + (C_3 + C_4 + ...)B^2 + ...\right)
\end{aligned}$$

i.e.

$$C(B) = C(1) + \Delta C^*(B) \quad (6.13)$$

where

$$C_j^* = -\sum_{i=j+1}^{\infty} C_i \qquad C_0^* = I_n - C(1)$$

Using (6.13), (6.12) becomes

$$\Delta y_t = C(1)\mu + C(1)\varepsilon_t + \Delta C^*(B)\varepsilon_t$$

which, on 'integrating', becomes

$$y_t = \mu_1^* t + C(1)\sum_{j=0}^{t}\varepsilon_j + C^*(B)\varepsilon_t$$

where $\mu_1^* = C(1)\mu$. When Π is of reduced rank $n - r$ then, analogous to the VAR decomposition $\phi(1) = I_n + \beta\alpha'$, $C(1)$ will be of reduced rank r so that $C(1) = \gamma\delta'$, where γ and δ are both of rank r. Thus, on defining

$$\tau_t = \delta'\left(\mu t + \sum_{j=0}^{t}\varepsilon_j\right) = \delta'\mu + \tau_{t-1} + \delta'\varepsilon_t, \qquad c_t = C^*(B)\varepsilon_t$$

we have the 'common trends' representation

$$y_t = \gamma\tau_t + c_t \tag{6.14}$$
$$\tau_t = \delta'\mu + \tau_{t-1} + \delta'\varepsilon_t$$

which expresses y_t as a linear combination of r random walks – the common trends τ_t– plus some stationary 'transitory' components. Equation (6.14) may be regarded as a multivariate extension of the B–N decomposition introduced in chapter 3, subsection 3.5.2. However, as the products $\gamma\delta'$ and $\gamma\xi(\xi^{-1}\delta')$, for any nonsingular $(n - r) \times (n - r)$ matrix ξ, will both equal $C(1)$, δ is not uniquely defined so that the trends are also not uniquely defined without introducing additional identifying conditions.

In the same way that common trends appear in y_t when $C(1)$ is of reduced rank, common cycles appear if $C^*(B)$ is of reduced rank, since $c_t = C^*(B)\varepsilon_t$ is the cyclical component of y_t. The presence of common cycles requires that there are linear combinations of the elements of y_t that do not contain these cyclical components, just as the presence of common trends requires that there are linear combinations of $\mathbf{y}_t$ that do not contain trends, i.e., those stationary linear combinations that are the error corrections defined by the cointegrating vectors contained in α. Thus we require a set of, say, $n - s$ linearly independent vectors, gathered together in the $n \times (n - s)$ matrix φ, such that

$$\varphi' \mathbf{c}_t = \varphi' \mathbf{C}^*(B)\varepsilon_t = 0$$

in which case

$$\varphi' \mathbf{y}_t = \varphi' \gamma \tau_t$$

Such a matrix will exist if all the $\mathbf{C}_i^*$ have less than full rank and if $\varphi' \mathbf{C}_i^*$ for all i. Under these circumstances, $\mathbf{C}_i^* = \mathbf{G}\tilde{\mathbf{C}}_i$ for all i, where $\mathbf{G}$ is an $n \times s$ matrix having full column rank and $\tilde{\mathbf{C}}_i^*$ may not have full rank. The cyclical component can then be written as

$$\mathbf{c}_t = \mathbf{G}\tilde{\mathbf{C}}(B)\varepsilon_t = \mathbf{G}\tilde{\mathbf{c}}_t$$

so that the n-element cycle $\mathbf{c}_t$ can be written as linear combinations of an s-element cycle $\tilde{\mathbf{c}}_i$, thus leading to the common trend–common cycle representation

$$\mathbf{y}_t = \gamma \tau_t + \mathbf{G}\tilde{\mathbf{c}}_t \tag{6.15}$$

The number, $n - s$, of linearly independent cofeature vectors making up φ can be at most r, and these will be linearly independent of the cointegrating vectors making up α. This is a consequence of the fact that $\varphi' \mathbf{y}_t$, being the vector of common trends, is $I(1)$, whereas $\alpha' \mathbf{y}_t$, being the vector of error corrections, is $I(0)$.

An interesting special case of the representation (6.15) occurs when $r + s = n$. In these circumstances, $\mathbf{y}_t$ has the unique trend-cycle decomposition $\mathbf{y}_t = \mathbf{y}_t^\tau + \mathbf{y}_t^c$, where

$$\mathbf{y}_t^\tau = \Theta_2 \varphi' \mathbf{y}_t = \Theta_2 \varphi' \gamma \tau_t$$

contains the stochastic trends and

$$\mathbf{y}_t^c = \Theta_1 \alpha' \mathbf{y}_t = \Theta_1 \varphi' \alpha' \mathbf{c}_t$$

contains the cyclical components. Here

$$[\Theta_1 \quad \Theta_2] = \begin{bmatrix} \alpha' \\ \phi' \end{bmatrix}^{-1}$$

Note that y_t^c is a linear combination of the error correction terms $e_t = \alpha' y_t$. Since both y_t^c and y_t^τ are functions of α and φ, they can easily be calculated as simple linear combinations of y_t.

The common trend–common cycle representation (6.15) depends, of course, on the number of common trends and cycles, r and s, in the system. The number of common trends can be estimated by following standard procedures for determining the number of coin-tegrating vectors, $n - r$, in a VAR. Conditional on r, the number of common cycles may be selected either through a canonical correla-tion analysis requiring nonstandard testing procedures, or by directly incorporating, and subsequently testing, the restrictions into the VECM. With a chosen value of r, the VECM (6.11) is, with $\mu = 0$ for simplicity,

$$\Delta y_t = \Gamma(B)\Delta y_{t-1} + \beta e_{t-1} + \varepsilon_t \tag{6.16}$$

The cofeature matrix φ is identified only up to an invertible trans-formation, as any linear combination of the columns of φ will also be a cofeature vector. The matrix can therefore be rotated to have an $(n - s)$-dimensional identity submatrix

$$\varphi = \begin{bmatrix} I_{n-s} \\ \varphi_{s\times(n-s)}^* \end{bmatrix}$$

$\varphi'\Delta y_t$ can then be considered as $n - s$ 'pseudo-structural form' equa-tions for the first $n - s$-elements of Δy_t. The system can be completed by adding the unconstrained VECM equations for the remaining s equations of Δy_t to obtain the system

$$\begin{bmatrix} I_{n-s} & \varphi^{*'} \\ 0_{s\times(n-s)} & I_s \end{bmatrix}\Delta y_t = \begin{bmatrix} 0_{(n-s)\times(n(p-1)+n-r)} \\ \Gamma_1^* \ldots \Gamma_{p-1}^* \ \beta^* \end{bmatrix}\begin{bmatrix} \Delta y_{t-1} \\ \vdots \\ \Delta y_{t-p+1} \\ e_{t-1} \end{bmatrix} + \varepsilon_t \tag{6.17}$$

where Γ_1^* contains the last s rows of Γ_1, etc. The unrestricted VECM (6.16) has $n(n(p-1)+r)$ parameters, whereas the pseudo-structural model (6.17) has $sn-s^2$ parameters in the first $n-s$ equations and $s(n(p-1)+n-r)$ in the s equations which complete the system, so imposing $(n-s)(n-s-r+n(p-1))$ restrictions. The system (6.17) can be estimated by full information maximum likelihood (FIML) or some other simultaneous equation technique and a likelihood ratio statistic of the restrictions imposed by the s common cycles can then be constructed. Note that if $p=1$ and $r=n-s$, the system will be just identified and no test for common cycles is needed, for the system will necessarily have $n-r$ common cycles. As the lag order p increases, so the system will generally become overidentified and tests for common cycles become necessary.

Example 6.3: Common trends and cycles in the UK macroeconomy

In this example we extend Example 6.2 by considering output, consumption and investment interactions in the UK for the period 1855–2000, the data for which are shown in Figure 6.2. For this extended sample period, all three series are generated as $I(1)$ processes. On defining the vector $\mathbf{y}_t = (c_t, i_t, y_t)'$, a model selection strategy suggested that a VAR(2) was appropriate, so that the following VECM is considered

$$\Delta\mathbf{y}_t = \mu + \Pi\mathbf{y}_{t-1} + \Gamma\Delta\mathbf{y}_{t-1} + \varepsilon_t$$

Cointegration analysis establishes that there is one cointegrating vector, so that, with $n=3$, there are $r=2$ common trends and a single error correction that is estimated as

$$e_t = c_t + 0.384i_t - 1.484y_t - 2.862$$

The log likelihood associated with the fitted VECM

$$\Delta\mathbf{y}_t = \mu + \Pi\mathbf{y}_{t-1} + \beta e_{t-1} + \varepsilon_t$$

is 761.67. Since the maximum number of cofeature vectors is at most two, s must be at least one. Setting $s=2$ produces the pseudo-structural model

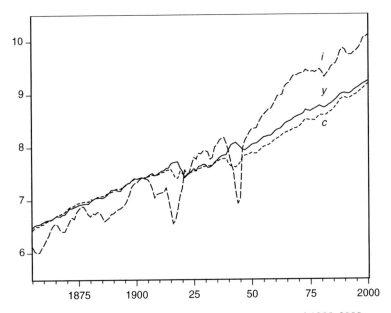

Figure 6.2 Output, consumption and income for the period 1855–2000

$$\Delta c_t = \mu_1 + \varphi_2 \Delta i_t + \varphi_3 \Delta y_t + \varepsilon_{1t}$$
$$\Delta i_t = \mu_2 + \gamma_{21} \Delta c_{t-1} + \gamma_{22} \Delta i_{t-1} + \gamma_{23} \Delta y_{t-1} + \beta_2 e_{t-1} + \varepsilon_{2t}$$
$$\Delta y_t = \mu_3 + \gamma_{31} \Delta c_{t-1} + \gamma_{32} \Delta i_{t-1} + \gamma_{33} \Delta y_{t-1} + \beta_3 e_{t-1} + \varepsilon_{3t}$$

while setting $s = 1$ produces

$$\Delta c_t = \mu_1 + \varphi_{13} \Delta y_t + \varepsilon_{1t}$$
$$\Delta i_t = \mu_2 + \varphi_{23} \Delta y_t + \varepsilon_{2t}$$
$$\Delta y_t = \mu_3 + \gamma_{31} \Delta c_{t-1} + \gamma_{32} \Delta i_{t-1} + \gamma_{33} \Delta y_{t-1} + \beta_3 e_{t-1} + \varepsilon_{3t}$$

The first model imposes 2 restrictions on the VECM, while the second imposes 6. Estimation of the two restricted models produces log likelihoods of 760.69 and 753.46, yielding test statistics $2(761.67 - 760.69) = 1.96$ and $2(761.67 - 753.46) = 16.42$. Since these are distributed as χ^2 with 2 and 6 degrees of freedom, respectively, $s = 2$ is selected. Estimating this model by FIML and deleting some insignificant coefficients obtains

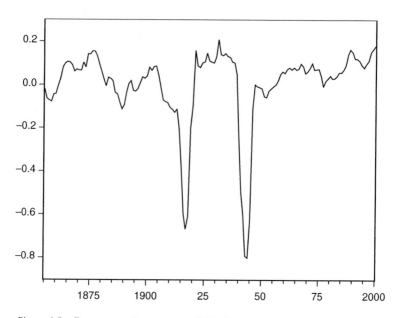

Figure 6.3   Error correction $e_t = c_t + 0.384i_t - 1.484y_t - 2.862$

$$\Delta c_t = 0.008 + 0.177\,\Delta i_t + 0.304\,\Delta y_t$$
$$\quad\;\; (0.003)\,(0.046)\qquad (0.157)$$

$$\Delta i_t = 0.851\Delta c_{t-1} + 0.372\,\Delta i_{t-1} - 0.161 e_{t-1}$$
$$\quad\;\; (0.422)\qquad\quad (0.066)\qquad\quad (0.032)$$

$$\Delta y_t = 0.015 - 0.042\,\Delta i_{t-1} + 0.282\,\Delta y_{t-1} + 0.061 e_{t-1}$$
$$\quad\;\; (0.003)\,(0.024)\qquad\quad (0.064)\qquad\quad (0.019)$$

The error correction e_t and the common cycle $\tilde{c}_t = \Delta c_t - 0.008 - 0.177\Delta i_t - 0.304\Delta y_t$ are shown in Figures 6.3 and 6.4. The former should be stationary, while the latter should be indistinguishable from white noise, which standard tests confirm. Noting that the weights attached to Δi_t and Δy_t are close to 1/6 and 1/3, the common cycle has the interpretation that the change in the linear combination $6c_t - i_t - 2y_t$ is white noise.

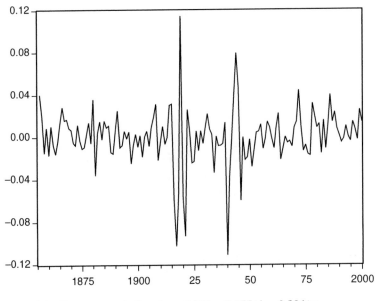

Figure 6.4   Common cycle $\tilde{c}_t = \Delta c_t - 0.008 - 0.177\Delta i_t - 0.304\Delta y_t$

6.3   Multivariate basic structural models

6.3.1   Common trends

The BSM introduced in Chapter 3, subsection 3.5.3, may be extended to the vector case. The simplest setup considers the decomposition $\mathbf{y}_t = \mu_t + \varepsilon_t$, where μ_t and ε_t are n-dimensional vectors of trends and cycles with ε_t being multivariate white noise with $n \times n$ covariance matrix Σ_ε. The trend is assumed to be

$$\mu_t = \mu_{t-1} + \beta_{t-1} + \eta_t \tag{6.18a}$$
$$\beta_t = \beta_{t-1} + \zeta_t \tag{6.18b}$$

where η_t and ζ_t are mutually uncorrelated multivariate white noises with covariance matrices Σ_η and Σ_ζ. The series making up $\mathbf{y}_t$ do not interact with each other in any causal sense, but may be subject to the same environment, so their movements are likely to be correlated. The permanent, or trend, movements in the series are linked by the off-diagonal elements of Σ_η, while short-run, or cyclical, movements depend on the off-diagonal elements of Σ_ζ. When $\Sigma_\eta = 0$, we obtain the multivariate version of the *smooth trend* model, while if $\Sigma_\zeta = 0$ the trend becomes a multivariate random walk with drift.

Suppose that $\Sigma_\zeta = 0$, so that $\beta_t = \beta_{t-1} = \beta$ and (6.18) becomes

$$\mu_t = \mu_{t-1} + \beta + \eta_t \tag{6.19}$$

We now assume that μ_t is a function of K_η common trends μ_t^*, so that $\mu_t = \Theta \mu_t^*$, where Θ is an $n \times K_\eta$ matrix of *standardised factor loadings*. The model then becomes

$$\begin{aligned}
\mathbf{y}_t &= \Theta \mu_t^* + \mu_0 + \varepsilon_t &\tag{6.20a}\\
\mu_t^* &= \mu_{t-1}^* + \beta^* + \eta_t &\tag{6.20b}
\end{aligned}$$

where $\beta = \Theta \beta^*$ and $\eta_t = \Theta \eta_t^*$. The new vector μ_0 in (6.20a) has zeros for its first K_η elements while its last $n - K_\eta$ elements are unconstrained constants. If the covariance matrix of η_t^* is D_η, then $\Sigma_\eta = \Theta D_\eta \Theta'$ will then be of rank $K_\eta < n$. Since $\Theta \mu_t^*$ can always be written as $\Theta \Xi \Xi^{-1} \mu_t^*$, where Ξ is a non-singular $K_\eta \times K_\eta$ matrix, we can define new factor loadings $\Theta^{**} = \Theta \Xi^{-1}$ and common trends $\mu_t^{**} = \Xi \mu_t^*$ that produce a model that is indistinguishable from (6.20). To ensure identifiability we can set D_η to a diagonal matrix and also restrict Θ. If the ijth element of Θ is θ_{ij}, then a set of identification restrictions are $\theta_{ii} = 1$ and $\theta_i = 0$ for $j > i$.

Requiring D_η to be diagonal is useful, as it means that the common trends are uncorrelated with each other. The restrictions on Θ are less appealing, since the block triangularity forces a causal structure onto the model: y_{1t} depends only on the first common trend, y_{2t} depends only on the first two common trends, and so on until we reach the K_ηth series, which depends on all the common trends, as do the remaining $n - K\eta$ series. This is clearly arbitrary and defining the trends in this way may not allow them to be easily interpreted. A possible solution is to use an orthogonal Ξ matrix to give a *factor rotation*, producing new trends μ_t^{**} that may be more easy to interpret.

Stochastic slopes, which may themselves be common, can also be included. In this case Σ_ζ will have rank $K_\zeta < n$ and the model becomes

$$\mu_t = \mu_{t-1} + \Theta_\beta \beta^*_{t-1} + \beta_\theta + \eta_t \tag{6.21a}$$
$$\beta^*_t = \beta^*_{t-1} + \zeta^*_t \tag{6.21b}$$

where Θ_β is an $n \times K_\zeta$ matrix such that $\Sigma_\zeta = \Theta_\beta D_\zeta \Theta'_\beta$, where D_ζ is the covariance matrix of the K_ζ-vector ζ^*_t, and β_θ is defined analogously to μ_0 in (6.20a).

6.3.2 Common cycles

The specification of the component ε_t can be generalised to incorporate a specific cycle. Analogous to (3.63), this is

$$\begin{bmatrix} \varepsilon_t \\ \varepsilon^*_t \end{bmatrix} = \left\{ \rho \begin{bmatrix} \cos\lambda_c & \sin\lambda_c \\ -\sin\lambda_c & \cos\lambda_c \end{bmatrix} \otimes I_n \right\} \begin{bmatrix} \varepsilon_t \\ \varepsilon^*_t \end{bmatrix} + \begin{bmatrix} s_t \\ s^*_t \end{bmatrix} \tag{6.22}$$

The vectors s_t and s^*_t are independent multivariate white noises with common covariance matrix Σ_s, while the parameters ρ and λ_c are the same for all series, so that their cycles have identical properties. This restriction allows for the possibility of common cycles: a model with common trends and cycles can be written as

$$y_t = \Theta_\mu \mu^*_t + \mu_0 + \Theta_\varepsilon \varepsilon_t$$

where Θ_ε is an $n \times K_\varepsilon$ matrix defined such that $\Sigma_\varepsilon = \Theta_\varepsilon D_\kappa \Theta'_\varepsilon$.

Example 6.4: A multivariate BSM of the UK macroeconomy

The consumption, investment and output data of Example 6.3 is now analysed within the framework of the multivariate BSM. An unrestricted model with trend given by (6.18) and cycle given by (6.22) was first fitted, leading to the estimated covariance matrices (the upper diagonal elements in italics are the estimated correlations)

$$\hat{\Sigma}_\eta = \begin{bmatrix} 4.57 \times 10^{-4} & -0.209 & 0.746 \\ -2.41 \times 10^{-4} & 2.92 \times 10^{-3} & 0.496 \\ 2.65 \times 10^{-4} & 4.45 \times 10^{-4} & 2.75 \times 10^{-4} \end{bmatrix}$$

$$\hat{\Sigma}_\zeta = \begin{bmatrix} 8.04 \times 10^{-6} & 0.821 & -0.583 \\ 6.23 \times 10^{-5} & 7.14 \times 10^{-4} & -0.942 \\ -6.89 \times 10^{-6} & -1.05 \times 10^{-4} & 1.74 \times 10^{-5} \end{bmatrix}$$

and

$$\hat{\Sigma}_s = \begin{bmatrix} 1.11 \times 10^{-4} & 0.892 & -0.412 \\ 5.88 \times 10^{-4} & 3.93 \times 10^{-3} & -0.248 \\ -6.86 \times 10^{-5} & -2.46 \times 10^{-4} & 2.50 \times 10^{-4} \end{bmatrix}$$

The estimates of the cycle parameters are $\hat{\rho} = 0.89$ and $\hat{\lambda}_c = 0.55$, implying stationary cyclical components having a common cyclical period of 11.5 years, and the overall log likelihood of the model is 1356.30.

There is no indication from these matrices that either of the levels or slopes covariance matrices are null. However, given the knowledge from Figure 6.2 and Example 6.3 that consumption and output have similar growth rates and cycles, the ranks of the Σ_ζ and Σ_s matrices were set at $K_\zeta = K_s = 2$. The restricted model has a log likelihood of 1356.26 and so the two parameter restrictions imposed by the rank conditions would appear to be acceptable. The restricted model thus takes the form

$$\mathbf{y}_t = \mu_t + \Theta_\varepsilon \varepsilon_t$$

where

$$\mu_t = \mu_{t-1} + \Theta_\beta \beta_{t-1}^* + \beta_\theta + \eta_t$$
$$\beta_t^* = \beta_{t-1}^* + \zeta_t^*$$

with estimated matrices

$$\hat{\Theta}_\beta = \begin{bmatrix} 1 & 0 \\ 7.74 & 1 \\ -0.85 & -0.22 \end{bmatrix} \quad \hat{\beta}_\theta = \begin{bmatrix} 0 \\ 0 \\ 0.0087 \end{bmatrix} \quad \hat{D}_\zeta = \begin{bmatrix} 0.0028 & 0 \\ 0 & 0.0155 \end{bmatrix}$$

$$\hat{\Theta}_\varepsilon = \begin{bmatrix} 1 & 0 \\ 6.01 & 1 \\ -0.65 & 1.70 \end{bmatrix} \quad \hat{D}_\kappa = \begin{bmatrix} 0.0101 & 0 \\ 0 & 0.0084 \end{bmatrix}$$

and parameters $\hat{\rho} = 0.89$ and $\hat{\lambda}_c = 0.54$, which are almost identical to the unrestricted estimates.

How can this model be interpreted? Concentrating first on the slope components, the relationship $\beta = \Theta\beta^*$ implies that, on incorporating β_θ,

$$\beta_{1t} = \beta_{1t}^*$$
$$\beta_{2t} = 7.74\beta_{1t}^* + \beta_{2t}^*$$
$$\beta_{3t} = -0.85\beta_{1t}^* - 0.22\beta_{2t}^* + 0.0087$$

Solving this system for β_{2t} in terms of β_{1t} and β_{3t} yields

$$\beta_{2t} = 3.86\beta_{1t} - 4.55\beta_{3t} + 0.0395$$

Thus, if consumption and output are growing at their sample mean rates of 1.9 per cent, investment will be growing at 2.7 per cent, which is approximately its sample mean growth rate.

By a similar route, the link between the three cyclical components can be calculated to be $\varepsilon_{2t} = 6.4\varepsilon_{1t} + 0.6\varepsilon_{3t}$, reflecting the fact that the variability and amplitude of the investment cycle is much greater that those of the cycles for consumption and output: see the estimated cycles shown in Figure 6.5.

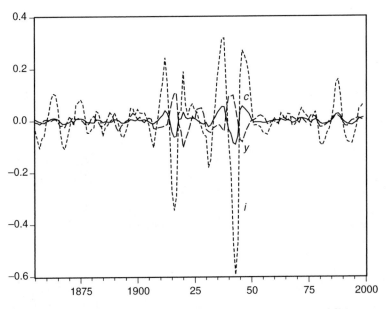

Figure 6.5 Cyclical components estimated from the multivariate BSM

6.4   Multivariate filtering

The univariate $H–P$ filter discussed in Chapter 4, section 4.2, results from minimising the expression

$$\sum_{t=1}^{T}(y_t - \mu_t)^2 + \lambda(c(B)\mu_t)^2 \tag{6.23}$$

with respect to μ_t, where $c(B) = (B^{-1}-1) - (1 - B)$. This yields the trend extraction filter

$$b_{H-P}(B) = \left(1 + \lambda(1 - B)^2(1 - B^{-1})^2\right)^{-1} = \left(1 + \lambda F(B)\right)^{-1}$$

and the extracted trend

$$\mu_t = \left(1 + \lambda F(B)\right)^{-1} y_t$$

Consider now the vector $\mathbf{y}_t = (y_{1t}, \dots, y_{nt})'$, where we assume that in the multivariate decomposition $\mathbf{y}_t = \mu_t + \varepsilon_t$ the n trend components μ_{it}, $i = 1, \dots, n$, are functions of a single common trend μ_t, so that $\mu_{it} = \gamma_i\mu_t$, where the γ_i, $i = 1, \dots, n$, are constants. The analogous multivariate minimisation problem to (6.23) is

$$\sum_{t=1}^{T}(\mathbf{y}_t - \gamma\mu_t)'A(\mathbf{y}_t - \gamma\mu_t) + \lambda(c(B)\mu_t)^2 \tag{6.24}$$

where $\gamma = (\gamma_1, \dots, \gamma_n)'$ and A is an $n \times n$ weighting matrix. Whereas γ may be based on economic theory, A is arbitrary, so that there is some flexibility in defining the trends, since the relative sizes of the elements of A determine which elements of $\mathbf{y}_t$ are more heavily weighted in the solution to (6.24). For example, if one of the series is considered to be less reliable than the others, less weight could be put on the deviations of this variable from trend. An extreme choice of A would be all zero elements except for a single nonzero diagonal entry, so defining the common trend to be the trend of just one of the series. A more general choice would make A proportional to the inverse of the covariance matrix of innovations to $\mathbf{y}_t$ or detrended $\mathbf{y}_t$.

A trade-off clearly exists between A and λ in (6.24). For example, for any constant $c > 0$, identical trends are obtained from the choice of $A = cA_0$ and $\lambda = \lambda_0$ or $A = A_0$ and $\lambda = \lambda_0/c$. This link between A and

λ can be developed further by noting that, on solving the minimisation problem (6.24), the multivariate H–P trend extraction filter is given by

$$\mu_t = \left(1 + \lambda F(B)\right)^{-1} \left(\gamma' A \gamma\right)^{-1} \gamma' A \mathbf{y}_t$$

If we adopt the normalisation $\gamma' A \gamma = 1$, this simplifies to

$$\mu_t = \left(1 + \lambda F(B)\right)^{-1} \gamma' A \mathbf{y}_t \qquad (6.25)$$

so that the same filter, $(1 + \gamma F(B))^{-1}$, defines the trend in both the univariate and multivariate cases, although since it operates on y_t in the former and $\gamma' A \mathbf{y}_t$ in the latter, trend estimates of the individual series will generally differ. Since (6.25) can also be written as

$$\mu_t = \gamma' A \left(1 + \lambda F(B)\right)^{-1} \mathbf{y}_t$$

two equivalent computational approaches may be taken to estimate the common trend. Either the univariate *H–P* filter can be applied to the series $\gamma' A \mathbf{y}_t$, or each of the individual series can be *H–P* filtered, to yield $\tilde{\mathbf{y}}_t = (1 + \lambda F(B))^{-1} \mathbf{y}_t$, and then $\mu_t = \gamma' A \tilde{\mathbf{y}}_t$ calculated. The detrended series is then calculated as

$$\varepsilon_t = \mathbf{y}_t - \gamma \mu_t = \mathbf{y}_t - \gamma \gamma' A \tilde{\mathbf{y}}_t$$

A more general formulation of the common trend is to introduce deterministic components:

$$\mu_{it} = d_{it}(t) + \gamma_t \mu_t$$

In this case the common trend is defined as

$$\mu_t = \left(1 + \lambda F(B)\right)^{-1} \gamma' A \left(\mathbf{y}_t - \mathbf{d}_t(t)\right)$$

where $\mathbf{d}_t(t) = (d_{1t}(t), \ldots, d_{nt}(t))'$. The simplest approach to trend construction is to first remove the deterministic trend components $\mathbf{d}_t(t)$ from the data and then estimate the common trend by applying the filter to the appropriate linear combination of the deterministically detrended data.

Example 6.5: Multivariate detrending of UK consumption and output using a common trend restriction

In this example we concentrate on just consumption and output for the UK for the period 1855–2000, thus now defining $y_t = (c_t, y_t)'$. It can be shown that the two series are cointegrated, so that they do indeed share a common trend, as suggested by standard theories of economic growth. Since the mean growth rates of the two series are both 1.9 per cent per annum, this suggests setting $\gamma = (1, 1)'$. As the growth rates of the two series have similar standard deviations (2.8 per cent and 3.1 per cent) and have a correlation in the order of 0.1, the weighting matrix was set at $A = 0.5I_2$, thus assuming that the deviations of each series from trend are equally weighted in defining the common trend. Note that $\gamma'A = (0.5, 0.5)$ and that these settings satisfy the identifying normalisation $\gamma'A\gamma = 1$. From Figure 6.2, consumption and output have common trends differing only by a constant, reflecting the different scalings of the original data. We thus assume that $\mu_{it} = d_i + \mu_t$, $i = 1, 2$, and estimate these constants by the respective sample means: $\hat{d}_1 = 7.709$ and $\hat{d}_2 = 4.789$.

Demeaned consumption and output, i.e., $\hat{c}_t = c_t - \hat{d}_1$ and $\hat{y}_t = y_t - \hat{d}_2$, were then H–P filtered using a smoothing parameter of $\lambda = 10$, yielding $\tilde{c}_t$ and $\tilde{y}_t$. The common trend is then given by $\mu_t = 0.5(\tilde{c}_t + \tilde{y}_t)$ and the detrended series by $\varepsilon_{1t} = \hat{c}_t - \mu_t$ and $\varepsilon_{1t} = \hat{y}_t - \mu_t$. The demeaned series and the common trend are shown in Figure 6.6, while the detrended, cyclical, components are shown in Figure 6.7, along with the cycles obtained from univariate detrending, i.e., $\hat{c}_t - \tilde{c}_t$ and $\hat{y}_t - \tilde{y}_t$, for comparison. Because the common trend is a weighted average of the two univariate trends, it is much smoother, and hence the cyclical components are more volatile than those produced by univariate detrending.

An interesting implication of the common trend in consumption and output is that the volatility of the logarithm of consumption's share in output should remain unaltered by detrending. This is easily seen by noting that

$$c_t - y_t = d_1 + \mu_t + \varepsilon_{1t} - d_2 - \mu_t - \varepsilon_{2t}$$
$$= d_1 - d_2 + \varepsilon_{1t} - \varepsilon_{2t}$$

so that the standard deviation of $\varepsilon_{1t} - \varepsilon_{2t}$ is the same as that of $c_t - y_t$. This, of course, is the case for the estimated standard deviation of

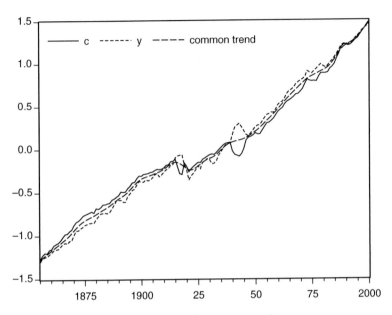

Figure 6.6 Consumption, output and common trend

the common detrended consumption share, which is 0.103. However, the standard deviation of the univariate detrended share is only 0.030, with the discrepancy being the standard deviation in the difference between the univariate trends in consumption and output, which would be zero if they shared a common trend.

Further reading and background material

6.1 Engle and Kozicki (1993) is the standard reference to common features, although related concepts had been developed earlier by, for example, Velu, Reinsel and Wichern (1986) and Ahn and Reinsel (1988).

6.2 The common trends framework within a VAR specification was initially developed by Stock and Watson (1988). Vahid and Engle (1993) extended the VAR framework to contain both common trends and cycles and proposed a test for common cycles that is based on the canonical correlation approach of

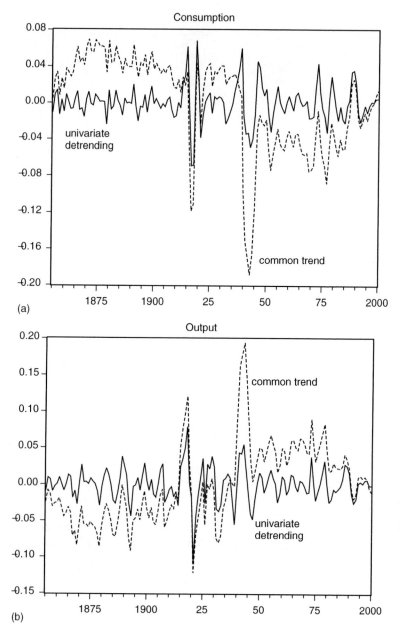

Figure 6.7 Cyclical components for consumption and output

Tiao and Tsay (1985) which, unfortunately, requires specialised computer algorithms for its calculation. Vahid and Engle (1997) extend the model further to include codependent cycles. Empirical applications include Engle and Issler (1995), Issler and Vahid (2001), Vahid and Issler (2002), and Harvey and Mills (2002b), while Mills (1998) is a useful expository article. Related decomposition techniques are proposed by Quah (1992) and Gonzalo and Granger (1995).

6.3 Aspects of multivariate Basic Structural Models are discussed in detail in Harvey (1989, 1993), which extend the initial work of Jones (1966). Applications to trends and cycles are still rare, perhaps because specific software is required. The *STAMP* package (see Koopman *et al.*, 2000) contains a full set of routines and the interested reader is referred to this for a complete development of the computational issues involved and numerous applied examples.

6.4 The idea of using filters under common trend restrictions is due to Kozicki (1999), where a detailed empirical example is provided.

7
Conclusions

The previous chapters have introduced a variety of methods for modelling trends and cycles in economic time series, ranging from simple deterministic linear trends and moving averages to multivariate structural models that incorporate reduced rank restrictions between components. What should the researcher do in practice? This, of course, is difficult to answer unless the economic problem that is being considered is fully articulated, but some general guidelines do suggest themselves. Perhaps the most important is the simplest – inspect the data using the full range of graphical techniques and summary statistics that are now available in econometric packages. While we have focused on graphical aspects here, we would also emphasise the importance of all types of 'exploratory data analysis', which includes data cleaning and a full understanding of the data collection process itself. Indeed, this should be the initial step in *any* empirical analysis, and it is one of the few things that Kennedy (2002) and Hendry (2002) seem to agree upon in their views on how to carry out applied econometrics!

If the aim of the research is primarily a descriptive decomposition into trend and cycle, which is often the case in historical exercises where a long time span is involved and where any underlying model structure tends to evolve through time, then using a filter would seem the best option, preferably a band pass or Butterworth. For shorter time spans, typically using data observed more frequently than annually, then there is no substitute for a detailed examination of the underlying stochastic process generating the data. This should be able to determine the type of trend model that should be considered: deterministic, stochastic, linear or nonlinear. If several series are being analysed together, then a VAR framework in which the presence of common trends and cycles can be examined would seem to be the appropriate choice of model, particularly if some economic theory can be brought to bear on the problem.

It should not be thought, however, that the behaviour of, in particular, trends is currently well understood by economists. Phillips, for example, argues that the converse is nearer the case: '[s]ince the early 1980s, a good deal of time-series econometrics has dealt with nonstationarity. The preoccupation has steadily become a central concern and it seems destined to continue, if only for the good empirical reason that most macroeconomic aggregates and financial time series are dominated by trend-like and random wandering behaviour. *Behaviour, it should be said, that is very imperfectly understood'* (Phillips, 2001, p. 21, emphasis added). Phillips goes on to ask, when faced with the evidence of continual structural change in the economy, and in particular the productivity growth shift of the late 1990s in the US, '[h]ow do we model trends when such fundamental changes are taking place? Reliance on a constant polynomial trend seems naïve and misplaced (yet compare the empirical evidence many researchers find favoring a trend stationary representation of real GDP). Use of a stochastic trend with a constant drift seems better because an upward drift in productivity can be captured by a series of positive innovations, but also seems unsatisfactory because the sources of change remain mysterious and their implications for policy obscure ... [W]e might seek to model the change by a trend break. But ... the chances of modelling it adequately using a break in a linear trend are naïvely optimistic. Unit roots and trend breaks do not explain the phenomenon, they simply account for it through the effect of a persistent shock, or by resetting initial conditions fro the trend. *Simply put, the inadequacy of our modelling apparatus in the face of an issue of such great importance is staggering'* (Phillips, 2001, p. 23, emphasis added).

Even taking into account the more recent evidence that the US productivity shift seems not have proved permanent, these remarks suggest that the modelling of trends, and by implication (and residual) that of cycles, will remain a crucial issue in econometric modelling for the foreseeable future. Indeed, Phillips (2001) makes several proposals that have the potential for forming the research agenda in this field for many years to come.

Computed Examples

Here we provide details of how several of the examples throughout the book were computed using the econometric software package *Econometric Views 4* (EViews). Although a basic knowledge of EViews is assumed, the examples are designed to allow many of the most useful commands to be used. Separate EViews workfiles are provided for each example.

Example 2.2: fitting deterministic trends to UK output

In EViews, load the workfile example 2.2.wf1, which contains annual observations from 1855 to 1999 on output, denoted gdp. The following commands will produce the series that are plotted in Figures 2.2 and 2.3:

```
genr y = log(gdp)
genr t = @trend
ls y c t ar(1) ar(2)
genr mulin = c(1) + c(2)*t
```

This will generate the series y and μ_{lin} that are plotted in Figure 2.2. Issuing the commands

```
smpl 1855 1918
genr d2 = 0
smpl 1919 1999
genr d2 = 1
```

151

```
smpl 1855 1999
genr td2 = t*d2
ls y c t d2 td2 ar(1) ar(2)
smpl 1855 1918
genr mu1 = c(1) + c(2)*t + c(3)*d2 + c(4)*td2
smpl 1919 1999
genr mu2 = c(1) + c(2)*t + c(3)*d2 + c(4)*td2
```

will produce the 'separate trends' equation and the series μ_1 and μ_2 that are plotted in Figure 2.3. To obtain the segmented linear trend, μ_{seg}, plotted in Figure 2.4, issue the sequence of commands:

```
genr psi2 = 0
genr psi3 = 0
smpl 1919 1999
genr psi2 = t - (1918 - 1855)
smpl 1922 1999
genr psi3 = t - (1921 - 1855)
smpl 1855 1999
ls y c t psi2 psi3 ar(1) ar(2)
genr museg = c(1) + c(2)*t + c(3)*psi2 + c(4)*psi3
```

The following command will produce the smooth transition equation, although care needs to be taken when choosing initial parameter values:

```
ls  y  =  c(1)  +  c(2)*t  +  (c(3)  +  c(4)*t)/(1  +
exp(-c(5)*(t - 145*c(6)))))
```

One possibility is to set the initial values to zero with the command:

```
param c(1) 0 c(2) 0 c(3) 0 c(4) 0 c(5) 0 c(6) 0
```

Alternatively, double click on the coefficient vector c in the workfile directory, put the spreadsheet view of the coefficients into edit mode, and then set them to zero. Close the coefficient vector window and issue the ls command above: convergence should be achieved after 480 iterations.

Example 2.6: the cyclical component of UK output

The cyclical component is obtained as the residual from the fitted smooth transition equation in Example 2.2. A simple way of generating the component is by the command (assuming that this is the last equation estimated):

```
genr cycle = resid
```

An AR(3) process can be fitted to the component by the command:

```
ls cycle ar(1) ar(2) ar(3)
```

noting that, because cycle has zero mean by definition, a constant is not needed. Examination of the regression output will reveal that the `ar(2)` coefficient is insignificant, so that the model can be reestimated as

```
ls cycle ar(1) ar(3)
```

The roots of the AR polynomial are shown at the bottom of the regression output.

Examples 3.2 and 3.4: modelling the *FTA All Share* Index

Load the workfile `example 3.2.wf1`, which contains the index itself, denoted `price`, and a time trend, denoted t, for the period 1965.01 to 1999.12. Generate the logarithms of the index and their differences by issuing the commands

```
genr p = log(price)
genr dp = d(p)
```

The AR(3) model for dp is obtained by either

```
ls dp c dp(-1) dp(-2) dp(-3)
```

which produces the reported regression, or

```
ls dp c ar(1) ar(2) ar(3)
```

which provides an estimate of the mean μ directly.

The ADF regression can be obtained by adding the regressors t and p(-1) to the above regression:

```
ls dp c t p(-1) dp(-1) dp(-2) dp(-3)
```

and examining the *t*-statistic on p(-1). Alternatively, click on p/view/unit root test, select the appropriate settings and the above equation will be run, the τ_τ statistic will be calculated and compared to the appropriate critical values, and a prob-value will be reported.

Example 4.5: band-pass and Hodrick–Prescott cycles for US output

Load the workfile example 4.5.wf1, which contains the logarithms of US output, denoted y. The $BP_{12}(6, 32)$ cycle can be calculated by issuing the command:

```
bp = 0.2777*y + (0.2204*(y(-1) + y(1))
+ 0.0838*(y(-2) + y(2)) - 0.0521*(y(-3) + y(3))
- 0.1184*(y(-4) + y(4)) - 0.1012*(y(-5) + y(5))
- 0.0422*(y(-6) + y(6)) + 0.0016*(y(-7) + y(7))
+ 0.0015*(y(-8) + y(8)) - 0.0279*(y(-9) + y(9))
- 0.0501*(y(-10) + y(10)) - 0.0423*(y(-11) + y(11))
- 0.0119*(y(-12) + y(12))
```

using the weights shown in Table 4.1. The H–$P(1000)$ cycle can be calculated by clicking on y/procs/hodrick–prescott filter. Select the appropriate value of the smoothing parameter and the name for the H–P trend, the default for which is hptrend01. The H–P cycle can then be calculated as:

```
genr hpcycle = y - hptrend01
```

Example 5.2: a STAR model for UK output

Load the workfile example 5.2.wk1, which contains the data on postwar quarterly UK output, denoted gdp. The analysis is performed using the first differences of the logarithms of gdp. These can be obtained directly by issuing the command:

```
genr dy = dlog(gdp)
```

Equation (5.12) with $p = 1$ and, initially, $k = 1$, is estimated by first setting up the variables

```
genr dy2 = dy^2
genr dy3 = dy^3
```

and then issuing the regression command:

```
ls dy = c(1) + c(2)*dy(-1) + c(3)*dy(-1)*dy(-1) +
c(4)*dy(-1)*dy2(-1) + c(5)*dy3(-1)
```

A test of H_0 is thus a test of $c(3) = c(4) = c(5) = 0$. This can be performed by clicking in the equation results window the sequence view/Coefficient Tests/Wald - Coefficient restrictions. Type in the restriction to be tested in the box and note the F-test prob-value of 0.038.

The testing sequence may then be repeated for $k = 2, 3, 4$ by restimating the equation

```
ls dy = c(1) + c(2)*dy(-1) + c(3)*dy(-1)*dy(-k) +
c(4)*dy(-1)*dy2(-k) + c(5)*dy3(-k)
```

for those values of k. Having selected $k = 4$, a test of $H_0^{(4)}$ is thus a t-test of the significance of $c(5)$, yielding the prob-value of 0.092. Conditional on $c(5) = 0$, $H_0^{(3)}$ is tested by running the regression

```
ls dy = c(1) + c(2)*dy(-1) + c(3)*dy(-1)*dy(-4) +
c(4)*dy(-1)*dy2(-4)
```

and using a t-test of the significance of $c(4)$, and repeating the sequence in an obvious manner provides a test of $H_0^{(2)}$.

The ESTAR model is fitted by

```
ls dy = c(1) + c(2)*(1 - exp(-c(5)*(dy(-4) -
c(6))^2)) + (c(3) + c(4)*(1 - exp(-c(5)*(dy(-4) -
c(6))^2)))*dy(-1)
```

Convergence is difficult to obtain and slightly different results are obtained from different starting values. This reflects the fact that the equation is overparameterised, which can make successful nonlinear estimation problematic. The estimates of c(2) and c(6) are invariably significant, though, thus leading to the parsimonious specification:

```
ls dy = c(2)*(1 - exp(-c(5)*(dy(-4) - c(6))^2))
```

The analogous LSTAR model can be estimated in a similar fashion as

```
ls dy = c(2)/(1 + exp(-c(5)*(dy(-4) - c(6))))
```

Example 5.3: nonparametric trends in US stock prices

Load the workfile example 5.3.wk1, which contains annual data from 1871 to 2001 on the logarithms of the S&P 500 index and a time trend. Highlight the variables t and p (in that order), double click to set up a group, and then click the sequence view/graph/scatter/scatter with kernel fit. Check local polynomial and set to 3, check normal (Gaussian) kernel, check user specified bandwidth and set to 2, and choose a name for the fitted series, say pfit1. This produces a scatterplot of t and p with a local cubic polynomial having a normal kernel and a bandwidth set at 2 superimposed. This sequence can be repeated with the bandwidth changed to 10.7 and the fitted series saved as pfit2, say. By saving the fitted series, the plots shown in Figure 5.3 may be constructed. Taking the differences of these series produces the trend growth rates plotted in Figure 5.4.

Example 6.1: is there a common cycle in US and Canadian output?

Load the workfile example 6.1.wf1, which contains quarterly data on Canadian and US output growth from 1955 to 1999, denoted cangr and usgr, respectively. The commands

```
smpl 1957.4 1999.4
ls usgr c usgr(-1)
ls cangr c cangr(-1) cangr(-2)
```

will produce the two univariate equations. The following commands will allow the common cycle test to be calculated:

```
2sls usgr c cangr @ usgr(-1) usgr(-2) cangr(-1)
cangr(-2)
genr e = resid
ls e c usgr(-1) usgr(-2) cangr(-1) cangr(-2)
```

The first equation estimates (6.3) by 2SLS under $\lambda = 0$ and the appropriate definitions of x_t and w_t. The second equation is the regression of e_t on x_t and w_t and produces $R^2 = 0.02292$, which, with $T = 169$, produces the reported test statistic. The SACF of e_t can be seen by double-clicking on e, clicking view/correlogram and selecting the default of level.

Example 6.2: common trends in the Victorian economy

Load the workfile example 6.2.wf1, which contains annual observations from 1855 to 1913 on the logarithms of UK output, y, consumption, cons, and investment, i, plus the time trend t. (Note that c and con are reserved names in EViews.) The equation system can be estimated by clicking on objects/new object/system and inputting the commands

```
y = c(1) + c(2)*t + [ar(1) = c(3), ar(2) = c(4)]
cons = c(5) + c(6)*t + [ar(1) = c(7), ar(2) = c(8)]
i = c(9) + c(10)*t + [ar(1) = c(11), ar(2) = c(12)]
```

Click estimate, select Seemingly Unrelated Regression as the estimation method and press OK, on which the estimates of the system will appear. To test for a common trend, click view/Wald coefficient tests … . Type c(2)=c(6)=c(10) and press OK, thus producing the test statistic and prob-value.

To impose a common trend, click Spec and edit the specification to obtain

```
y = c(1) + c(2)*t + [ar(1) = c(3), ar(2) = c(4)]
cons = c(5) + c(2)*t + [ar(1) = c(7), ar(2) = c(8)]
i = c(9) + c(2)*t + [ar(1) = c(11), ar(2) = c(12)]
```

whereupon estimation can be repeated.

Example 6.3: common trends and cycles in the UK macroeconomy

Workfile example 6.3.wf1 contains the same variables as the previous workfile but for the longer sample period 1855 to 2000. After loading this workfile, click on the *main menu* Quick/Estimate VAR ... and keep the VAR Specification as it stands, apart from adding t to the exogenous variables list. Press OK and then click View/Lag structure/Lag length criteria ... . Select 8 as the lags to include and press OK. Various lag length selection criteria are shown, which select either a lag length of 2 or 3. Deciding on the former, click Estimate, check Vector error correction, change the Estimation sample to 1858 2000 (to maintain consistency with the results reported in the text), delete t from the exogenous variables list and press OK. The error correction is reported as CointEq1 and the log likelihood as one of the model's summary statistics.

The error correction is required for estimation of the pseudo-structural models needed to examine common cycles. This can be calculated by the command

```
genr ecm = cons + 0.384*i - 1.484*y - 2.862
```

The first pseudo-structural model is estimated by setting up the system

```
d(cons) = c(1) + c(2)*d(i) + c(3)*d(y)
d(i) = c(4) + c(5)*d(cons(-1)) + c(6)*d(y(-1))
+ c(7)*ecm(-1)
d(y) = c(8) + c(9)*d(cons(-1)) + c(10)*d(y(-1))
+ c(11)*ecm(-1)
```

and using Full Information Maximum Likelihood as the estimation method. The second pseudo-structural model can be estimated in an analogous fashion. Log likelihoods are part of the statistical output and can be used to calculate the common cycle test statistics. The restricted model reported in the text can be obtained by editing the system appropriately and reestimating.

Example 6.5: multivariate detrending of UK consumption and output using a common trend restriction

Continuing to use workfile `example 6.3.wf1`, the mean and standard deviations of the growth rates of consumption and output can be obtained by issuing the command

```
show d(cons) d(y)
```

and clicking `View/Descriptive Stats/Common sample` and reading off the means and standard deviations (remembering to multiply by 100 for percentages). The means of `cons` and `y` can be obtained in an analogous way. A direct way of calculating demeaned consumption and output is

```
genr cdm = cons - @mean(cons)
genr ydm = y - @mean(y)
```

The common trend and the various detrended series can then be obtained from the Hodrick–Prescott trends in an obvious fashion.

References

Ahn, S.K. and Reinsel, G.C. (1988), 'Nested reduced rank autoregressive models for multiple time series', *Journal of the American Statistical Association*, 83, 849–856.

Ames, E. (1948), 'A theoretical and statistical dilemma – the contribution of Burns, Mitchell, and Frickey to business-cycle theory', *Econometrica*, 16, 347–369.

Bacon, D.W. and Watts, D.G. (1971), 'Estimating the transition between two intersecting straight lines', *Biometrika*, 58, 525–534.

Balke, N.S. and Fomby, T.B. (1991), 'Shifting trends, segmented trends, and infrequent permanent shocks', *Journal of Monetary Economics*, 28, 61–85.

Banerjee, A., Dolado, J., Galbraith, J.W. and Hendry, D.F. (1993), *Co-Integration, Error-Correction, and the Econometric Analysis of Non-Stationary Data*, Oxford: Oxford University Press.

Baumol, W.J. and Benhabib, J. (1989), 'Chaos: significance, mechanism, and economic applications', *Journal of Economic Perspectives*, 3(1), 77–105.

Baxter, M. and King, R.G. (1999), 'Measuring business cycles: approximate band-pass filters for economic time series', *Review of Economics and Statistics*, 81, 575–593.

Bell, W.R. (1984), 'Signal extraction for nonstationary time series', *Annals of Statistics*, 13, 646–664.

Beveridge, S. and Nelson, C.R. (1981), 'A new approach to decomposition of economic time series into permanent and transitory components with particular attention to measurement of the "business cycle"', *Journal of Monetary Economics*, 7, 151–174.

Beveridge, W.H. (1920), 'British exports and the barometer', *Economic Journal*, 30, 13–25.

Beveridge, W.H. (1921), 'Weather and harvest cycles', *Economic Journal*, 31, 429–452.

Box, G.E.P. and Jenkins, G.M. (1976), *Time Series Analysis: Forecasting and Control*, revised edition, San Francisco: Holden-Day.

Brock, W.A. and Sayers, C.L. (1988), 'Is the business cycle characterized by deterministic chaos?', *Journal of Monetary Economics*, 22, 71–90.

Brockwell, P.J. and Davis, R.A. (1991), *Time Series: Theory and Methods*, 2nd edition, New York, Springer-Verlag.

Burns, A.F. and Mitchell, W.C. (1946), *Measuring Business Cycles*, New York: National Bureau of Economic Research.

Burnside, C. (1998), 'Detrending and business cycle facts: a comment', *Journal of Monetary Economics*, 41, 513–532.

Canjels, E. and Watson, M.W. (1997), 'Estimating deterministic trends in the presence of serially correlated errors', *Review of Economics and Statistics*, 79, 184–200.

Canova, F. (1998), 'Detrending and business cycle facts', *Journal of Monetary Economics*, 41, 475–512.

Chan, K.H., Hayya, J.C. and Ord, J.K. (1977), 'A note on trend removal methods: the case of polynomial versus variate differencing', *Econometrica*, 45, 737–744.

Chan, K.S. and Tong, H. (1986), 'On estimating thresholds in autoregressive models', *Journal of Time Series Analysis*, 7, 179–190.

Cogley, T. and Nason, J.M. (1995), 'Effects of the Hodrick–Prescott filter on trend and difference stationary time series. Implications for business cycle research', *Journal of Economic Dynamics and Control*, 19, 253–278.

Craddock, J.M. (1957), 'An analysis of the slower temperature variations at Kew Observatory by means of exclusive bandpass filters', *Journal of the Royal Statistical Society*, 120, 387–397.

Crafts, N.F.R., Leybourne, S.J. and Mills, T.C. (1989), 'The climacteric in late Victorian and France: a reappraisal of the evidence', *Journal of Applied Econometrics*, 4, 103–117.

Crafts, N.F.R. and Mills, T.C (1994a), 'Trends in real wages in Britain, 1750–1913', *Explorations in Economic History*, 31, 176–194.

Crafts, N.F.R. and Mills, T.C. (1994b), 'The industrial revolution as a macro-economic epoch: an alternative view', *Economic History Review*, 47, 769–775.

Crafts, N.F.R. and Mills, T.C. (1997), 'Endogenous innovation, trend growth, and the British industrial revolution: reply to Greasley and Oxley', *Journal of Economic History*, 57, 950–956.

Cuddington, J.T. and Winters, A.L. (1987), 'The Beveridge–Nelson decomposition of economic time series: a quick computational method', *Journal of Monetary Economics*, 19, 125–127.

DeJong, D.N. and Whiteman, C.H. (1991), 'Reconsidering "Trends and random walks in macroeconomic time series"', *Journal of Monetary Economics*, 28, 221–254.

Dickey, D.A. and Fuller, W.A. (1979), 'Distribution of the estimators for autoregressive time series with a unit root', *Journal of the American Statistical Association*, 74, 427–431.

Diebold, F.X. and Rudebusch, G.D. (1990), 'A nonparametric investigation of duration dependence in the American business cycle', *Journal of Political Economy*, 98, 596–616.

Diebold, F.X. and Rudebusch, G.D. (1996), 'Measuring business cycles: a modern perspective', *Review of Economics ad Statistics*, 78, 67–77.

Engle, R.F. and Issler, J.V. (1995), 'Estimating common sectoral cycles', *Journal of Monetary Economics*, 35, 83–113.

Engle, R.F. and Kozicki, S. (1993), 'Testing for common features', *Journal of Business and Economic Statistics*, 11, 369–380.

Fisher, I. (1925), 'Our unstable dollar and the so-called business cycle', *Journal of the American Statistical Association*, 20, 179–202.

Frickey, E. (1934), 'The problem of secular trend', *Review of Economics and Statistics*, 16, 199–206.

Friedman, M. (1957), *A Theory of the Consumption Function*, Princeton: Princeton University Press.

Frisch, R. (1933), 'Propagation problems and impulse problems in dynamic economics', in *Economic Essays in Honour of Gustav Cassel*, London: George Allen & Unwin, 171–205.

Frisch, R. (1939), 'A note on errors in time series', *Quarterly Journal of Economics*, 53, 639–640.

Fuller, W.A. (1976), *Introduction to Statistical Time Series*, New York: Wiley.

Gonzalo, J. and Granger, C.W.J. (1995), 'Estimation of common long-memory components in cointegrated systems', *Journal of Business and Economic Statistics*, 13, 27–35.

Gourieroux, C. and Montfort, A. (1997), *Time Series and Dynamic Models*, Cambridge: Cambridge University Press.

Granger, C.W.J., Inoue, T. and Morin, N. (1997), 'Nonlinear stochastic trends', *Journal of Econometrics*, 81, 65–92.

Granger, C.W.J. and Newbold, P. (1986), *Forecasting Economic Time Series*, 2nd edition, San Diego: Academic Press.

Granger, C.W.J. and Teräsvirta, T. (1993), *Modelling Nonlinear Economic Relationships*, Oxford: Oxford University Press.

Greasley, D. (1986), 'British economic growth: the paradox of the 1880s and the timing of the climacteric', *Explorations in Economic History*, 23, 416–444.

Grenander, U. (1954), 'On the estimation of regression coefficients in the case of autocorrelated disturbances', *Annals of Mathematical Statistics*, 25, 252–272.

Haavelmo, T. (1943), 'Statistical testing of business-cycle theories', *Review of Economics and Statistics*, 25, 13–18.

Hamilton, J.D. (1989), 'A new approach to the economic analysis of nonstationary time series and the business cycle', *Econometrica*, 57, 357–384.

Hamilton, J.D. (1990), 'Analysis of time series subject to changes in regime', *Journal of Econometrics*, 45, 39–70.

Hamilton, J.D. (1994), *Time Series Analysis*, Princeton: Princeton University Press.

Härdle, W. (1990), *Applied Nonparametric Regression*, Cambridge: Cambridge University Press.

Harvey, A.C. (1985), 'Trends and cycles in macroeconomic time series', *Journal of Business and Economic Statistics*, 3, 216–227.

Harvey, A.C. (1989), *Forecasting, Structural Time Series Models and the Kalman Filter*, Cambridge: Cambridge University Press.

Harvey, A.C. (1993), *Time Series Models*, 2nd edition, London: Harvester Wheatsheaf.

Harvey, A.C. and Jaeger, A. (1993), 'Detrending, stylized facts, and the business cycle', *Journal of Applied Econometrics*, 8, 231–247.

Harvey, A.C. and Koopman, S. (2000), 'Signal extraction and the formulation of unobserved component models', *Econometrics Journal*, 1, 1–24.

Harvey, A.C. and Shephard, N. (1992), 'Structural time series models', in G.S. Maddala, C.R. Rao and H.D. Vinod (eds), *Handbook of Statistics, Volume XI: Econometrics*, Amsterdam: North-Holland.

Harvey, A.C. and Todd, P.H.J. (1983), 'Forecasting economic time series with structural and Box–Jenkins models (with discussion)', *Journal of Business and Economic Statistics*, 1, 299–315.

Harvey, D.I. and Mills, T.C. (2001), 'Modelling global temperature trends using cointegration and smooth transitions', *Statistical Modelling*, 1, 143–159.

Harvey, D.I. and Mills, T.C. (2002a), 'Unit roots and double smooth transitions', *Journal of Applied Statistics*, 29, 675–683.

Harvey, D.I. and Mills, T.C. (2002b), 'Common features in UK sectoral output', *Economic Modelling*, 19, 91–104.

Hendry, D.F. (2002), 'Applied econometrics without sinning', *Journal of Economic Surveys*, 16, 591–604.

Hendry, D.F. and Morgan, M.S. (1995), *The Foundations of Econometric Analysis*, Cambridge: Cambridge University Press.

Higgins, B. (1955), 'Interactions of cycles and trends', *Economic Journal*, 65, 589–614.

Hodrick, R.J. and Prescott, E.C. (1997), 'Postwar US business cycles: an empirical investigation', *Journal of Money, Credit and Banking*, 29, 1–16.

Hooker, R.H. (1901), 'Correlation of the marriage rate with trade', *Journal of the Royal Statistical Society*, 64, 485–503.

Issler, J.V. and Vahid, F. (2001), 'Common cycles and the importance of transitory shocks to macroeconomic aggregates', *Journal of Monetary Economics*, 47, 449–475.

Jones, R.H. (1966), 'Exponential smoothing for multivariate time series', *Journal of the Royal Statistical Society, Series B*, 28, 241–251.

Kaldor, N. (1940), 'A model of the trade cycle', *Economic Journal*, 50, 78–92.

Kaldor, N. (1954), 'The relation of economic growth and cyclical fluctuations', *Economic Journal*, 64, 53–71.

Kendall. M.G. (1973), *Time Series*, London: Charles Griffin.

Kennedy, P.E. (2002), 'Sinning in the basement: what are the rules? The ten commandments of applied econometrics', *Journal of Economic Surveys*, 16, 569–589.

Kenny, P.B. and Durbin, J. (1982), 'Local trend estimation and seasonal adjustment of economic and social time series (with discussion)', *Journal of the Royal Statistical Society, Series A*, 145, 1–41.

Keynes, J.M. (1939), 'Professor Tinbergen's method', *Economic Journal*, 49, 558–568.

Kim, C.J. and Nelson, C.R. (1999), *State–Space Models with Regime Switching: Classical and Gibbs-Sampling Approaches with Applications*, Cambridge, Mass.: MIT Press.

King, R.G. and Rebelo, S.T. (1993), 'Low frequency filtering and real business cycles', *Journal of Economic Dynamics and Control*, 17, 207–231.

Kitchin, J. (1923), 'Cycles and trends in economic factors', *Review of Economics and Statistics*, 5, 10–16.

Klein, J.L. (1997), *Statistical Visions in Time. A History of Time Series Analysis 1662–1938*, Cambridge: Cambridge University Press.

Klein, L.R. and Kosobud, R.F. (1961), 'Some econometrics of growth: great ratios of economics', *Quarterly Journal of Economics*, 75, 173–198.

Koopman, S.J., Harvey, A.C., Doornik, J.A. and Shephard, N. (2000), *STAMP 6: Structural Time Series Analysis Modeller and Predictor*, London: Timberlake Consultants Ltd.

Koopman, S.J., Shephard, N. and Doornik, J.A. (1999), 'Statistical algorithms for models in state space using SsfPack 2.2', *Econometrics Journal*, 2, 113–166.

Koopmans, T.C. (1947), 'Measurement without theory', *Review of Economics and Statistics*, 29, 161–172.

Kozicki, S. (1999), 'Multivariate detrending under common trend restrictions: implications for business cycle research', *Journal of Economic Dynamics and Control*, 23, 997–1028.

Kuznets, S. (1929), 'Random events and cyclical oscillations', *Journal of the American Statistical Association*, 24, 258–275.

Kydland, F.E. and Prescott, E.C. (1982), 'Time to build and aggregate fluctuations', *Econometrica*, 50, 1345–1370.

Lam, P.-S. (1990), 'The Hamilton model with a general autoregressive component: estimation and comparison with other models of economic time series', *Journal of Monetary Economics*, 20, 409–432.

Leybourne, S.J., Newbold, P. and Vougas, D. (1998), 'Unit roots and smooth transitions', *Journal of Time Series Analysis*, 19, 83–97.

Lippi, M. and Reichlin, L. (1992), 'On persistence of shocks to economic variables. A common misconception', *Journal of Monetary Economics*, 29, 87–93.

Lo, A.W., Mamaysky, H. and Wang, J. (2000), 'Foundations of technical analysis: computational algorithms, statistical inference, and empirical implementation', *Journal of Finance*, 55, 1705–1765.

Long, J.B. and Plosser, C.I. (1983), 'Real business cycles', *Journal of Political Economy*, 91, 39–69.

Lucas, R.E. (1975), 'An equilibrium model of the business cycle', *Journal of Political Economy*, 83, 1113–1144.

Maddala, G.S. and Kim, I.-M. (1998), *Unit Roots, Cointegration and Structural Change*, Cambridge: Cambridge University Press.

Metzler, L.A. (1941), 'The nature and stability of inventory cycles', *Review of Economics and Statistics*, 23, 113–129.

Miller, S.M. (1988), 'The Beveridge–Nelson decomposition of economic time series: another economical computational method', *Journal of Monetary Economics*, 21, 141–142.

Mills, T.C. (1990), *Time Series Techniques for Economists*, Cambridge: Cambridge University Press.

Mills, T.C. (1998), 'Recent developments in modelling nonstationary vector autoregressions', *Journal of Economic Surveys*, 12, 279–312.

Mills, T.C. (1999), *The Econometric Modelling of Financial Time Series*, 2nd edition, Cambridge: Cambridge University Press.

Mills, T.C. (2002), *Long Term Trends and Business Cycles, Volumes I and II*, The International Library of Critical Writings in Economics, 149, Cheltenham: Edward Elgar.

Mills, T.C. and Crafts, N.F.R. (1996), 'Trend growth in British industrial output, 1700–1913: a reappraisal', *Explorations in Economic History*, 33, 277–295.

Mitchell, W.C. (1913), *Business Cycles and their Causes*, Berkeley: California University Memoirs, Vol. III.

Mitchell, W.C. (1927), *Business Cycles: The Problem and its Setting*, New York: National Bureau of Economic Research.

Morgan, M.S. (1990), *The History of Econometric Ideas*, Cambridge: Cambridge University Press.

Murray, C.J. and Nelson, C.R. (2000), 'The uncertain trend in US GDP', *Journal of Monetary Economics*, 46, 79–95.

Muth, J.F. (1960), 'Optimal properties of exponentially weighted forecasts', *Journal of the American Statistical Association*, 55, 299–305.

Neftçi, S.N. (1984), 'Are economic time series asymmetric over the business cycle?', *Journal of Political Economy*, 92, 307–328.

Nelson, C.R. and Kang, H. (1981), 'Spurious periodicity in inappropriately detrended time series', *Econometrica*, 49, 741–751.

Nelson, C.R. and Kang, H. (1984), 'Pitfalls in the use of time as an explanatory variable in regression', *Journal of Business and Economic Statistics*, 2, 73–82.

Nelson, C.R. and Plosser, C.I. (1982), 'Trends and random walks in macroeconomic time series: some evidence and implications', *Journal of Monetary Economics*, 10, 139–162.

Newbold, P. (1990), 'Precise and efficient computation of the Beveridge–Nelson decomposition of economic time series', *Journal of Monetary Economics*, 26, 453–457.

Newbold, P. and Vougas, D. (1996), 'Beveridge–Nelson-type trends for I(2) and some seasonal models', *Journal of Time Series Analysis*, 17, 151–169.

Nicolau, J. (2002), 'Stationary processes that look like random walks – the bounded random walk process in discrete and continuous time', *Econometric Theory*, 18, 99–118.

Niemira, M.P. and Klein, P.A. (1994), *Forecasting Financial and Economic Cycles*, New York: Wiley.

Nordhaus, W.D. (1975), 'The political business cycle', *Review of Economic Studies*, 42, 169–190.

Osborn, D.R. (1995), 'Moving average detrending and the analysis of business cycles', *Oxford Bulletin of Economics and Statistics*, 57, 547–558.

Pedersen, T.M. (2001), 'The Hodrick–Prescott filter, the Slutzky effect, and the distortionary effect of filters', *Journal of Economic Dynamics and Control*, 25, 1081–1101.

Perron, P. (1989), 'The Great Crash, the oil price shock and the unit root hypothesis', *Econometrica*, 57, 1361–1401.

Perron, P. (1997), 'Further evidence on breaking trend functions in macroeconomic variables', *Journal of Econometrics*, 80, 355–385.

Persons, W.M. (1923), 'Correlation of time series', *Journal of the American Statistical Association*, 18, 713–726.

Pierce, D.A. (1979), 'Signal extraction error in nonstationary time series', *Annals of Statistics*, 7, 1303–1320.

Phillips, P.C.B. (2001), 'Trending time series and macroeconomic activity: some present and future challenges', *Journal of Econometrics*, 100, 21–27.

Pollock, D.S.G. (1999), *A Handbook of Time -Series Analysis, Signal Processing and Dynamics*, San Diego: Academic Press.

Pollock, D.S.G. (2000), 'Trend estimation and de-trending via rational square wave filters', *Journal of Econometrics*, 99, 317–334.

Pollock, D.S.G. (2001a), 'Methodology for trend estimation', *Economic Modelling*, 18, 75–96.

Pollock, D.S.G. (2001b), 'Filters for short nonstationary sequences', *Journal of Forecasting*, 20, 341–355.

Poynting, J.H. (1884), 'A comparison of the fluctuations in the price of wheat and in cotton and silk imports into Great Britain', *Journal of the Royal Statistical Society*, 47, 34–74.

Proietti, T. and Harvey, A.C. (2000), 'A Beveridge–Nelson smoother', *Economics Letters*, 67, 139–146.

Quah, D. (1992), 'The relative importance of permanent and transitory components: identification and some theoretical bounds', *Econometrica*, 60, 107–118.

Rudebusch, G.D. (1992), 'Trends and random walks in macroeconomic time series: a reexamination', *International Economic Review*, 33, 661–680.

Samuelson, P.A. (1939), 'Interactions between the multiplier analysis and the principle of the accelerator', *Review of Economics and Statistics*, 21, 75–78.

Simonoff, J.S. (1996), *Smoothing Methods in Statistics*, New York: Springer.

Slutsky, E. ([1927] 1937), 'The summation of random causes as the source of cyclic processes', *Econometrica*, 5, 105–146 (translation from Russian).

Sollis, R., Leybourne, S.J. and Newbold, P. (1999), 'Unit roots and asymmetric smooth transitions', *Journal of Time Series Analysis*, 20, 671–677.

Solow, R.M. (1970), *Growth Theory*, New York: Oxford University Press.

Stock, J.H. (1987), 'Measuring business cycle time', *Journal of Political Economy*, 95, 1240–1261.

Stock, J.H. and Watson, M.W. (1988), 'Testing for common trends', *Journal of the American Statistical Association*, 83, 1097–1107.

Stock, J.H. and Watson, M.W. (1991), 'A probability model of the coincident economic indicators', in K. Lahiri and G.H. Moore (eds), *Leading Economic Indicators: New Approaches and Forecasting Records*, Cambridge: Cambridge University Press, 63–89.

Teräsvirta, T. (1994), 'Specification, estimation, and evaluation of smooth transition autoregressive models', *Journal of the American Statistical Association*, 89, 208–218.

Teräsvirta, T. (1998), 'Modelling economic relationships with smooth transition regressions', in A. Ullah and D.E.A. Giles (eds), *Handbook of Applied Economic Statistics*, New York: Marcel Dekker, 507–552.

Teräsvirta, T. and Anderson, H.M. (1992), 'Characterizing nonlinearities in business cycles using smooth transition autoregressive models', *Journal of Applied Econometrics*, 7, S119–S136.

Tiao, G.C. and Tsay, R.S. (1985), 'A canonical correlation approach to modelling multivariate time series', in *Proceedings of the Business and Economic Statistics Section, American Statistical Association*, 112–120.

Tinbergen, J. (1937), *An Econometric Approach to Business Cycle Problems*, Paris: Hermann & Cie.

Tinbergen, J. (1939a), *Statistical Testing of Business-Cycle Theories, Volume 1: A Method and its Application to Investment Activity*, Geneva: League of Nations.

Tinbergen, J. (1939b), *Statistical Testing of Business-Cycle Theories, Volume 1I: Business Cycles in the United States of America*, Geneva: League of Nations.

Tinbergen, J. (1940), 'On a method of statistical business-cycle research. A reply', *Economic Journal*, 50, 141–154.

Tinbergen, J. (1942), 'Critical remarks on some business-cycle theories', *Econometrica*, 10, 129–146.

Tinbergen, J. (1951), *Business Cycles in the United Kingdom 1870–1914*, Amsterdam: North-Holland.

Tong, H. and Lim, K.S. (1980), 'Threshold regressions, limit cycles, and data (with discussion)', *Journal of the Royal Statistical Society, Series B*, 42, 245–292.

Vahid, F. and Engle, R.F. (1993), 'Common trends and common cycles', *Journal of Applied Econometrics*, 8, 341–360.

Vahid, F. and Engle, R.F. (1997), 'Codependent cycles', *Journal of Econometrics*, 80, 199–221.

Vahid, F. and Issler, J.V. (2002), 'The importance of common cyclical features in VAR analysis: a Monte-Carlo study', *Journal of Econometrics*, 109, 341–363.

Varian, H. (1979), 'Catastrophe theory and the business cycle', *Economic Inquiry*, 17, 14–28.

Velu, R.P., Reinsel, G.C. and Wichern, D.W. (1986), 'Reduced rank models for multiple time series', *Biometrika*, 73, 105–118.

Vining, R. (1949), 'Methodological issues in quantitative economics', *Review of Economics and Statistics*, 31, 77–94.

Whittaker, E.T. (1923), 'On a new method of graduations', *Proceedings of the Edinburgh Mathematical Society*, 41, 63–75.

Whittle, P. (1983), *Prediction and Regulation*, 2nd edition, Oxford: Blackwell.

Yatchew, A. (1998), 'Nonparametric regression techniques in economics', *Journal of Economic Literature*, 36, 669–721.

Yule, G.U. (1921), 'On the time-correlation problem with especial reference to the variate-difference correlation method', *Journal of the Royal Statistical Society*, 84, 497–526.

Yule, G.U. (1926), 'Why do we sometimes get nonsense correlations between time-series? – A study in sampling and the nature of time series', *Journal of the Royal Statistical Society*, 89, 1–64.

Yule, G.U. (1927), 'On a method of investigating periodicities in disturbed series with special reference to Wolfer's sunspot numbers', *Philosophical Transactions*, 226, 267–298.

Zarnowitz, V. (1985), 'Recent work on business cycles in historical perspective: a review of theories and evidence', *Journal of Economic Literature*, 23, 523–580.

Zeeman, C. (1977), *Catastrophe Theory: Selected Papers 1972–1977*, Reading Mass.: Addison-Wesley.

Author Index

Subject Index